THE
FIRST CHARITY

The
First
Charity

How Philanthropy Can Contribute to Democracy in America

Robert Matthews Johnson

Foreword by James A. Joseph

Seven Locks Press
Cabin John, MD/Washington, DC

Library of Congress Cataloging-in-Publication Data

Johnson, Robert Matthews
  The First Charity: How Philanthropy Can Contribute to Democracy
  in America.

  p. cm.
  Bibliography: p.
  Includes index.

  1. Charities—United States.   2. Philanthropists—United States.
    3. Democracy.   I. Title.
HV91.J626   1988
361.7'0973—dc19   88-11324
ISBN 0-932020-53-4 (pbk.)   CIP

Design by Giles Bayley
Cover by Betsy Bayley
Typesetting by Bets LTD

Printing by Sheridan Press

Manufactured in the United States of America.

First edition, July 1988

Printed on acid-free paper.

SEVEN LOCKS PRESS
P.O. Box 27
Cabin John, MD 20818
(301) 320-2130

To Chris, Craig, and Nick

Contents

Acknowledgments

Research and writing for *The First Charity* was made possible by a fellowship from the Public Affairs Program of the College of the University of Chicago, funded by the Spencer and Joyce foundations. I am immensely grateful to Thomas James and Marion Faldet of the Spencer Foundation, to Charles Daly and Craig Kennedy of the Joyce Foundation, and to their boards of directors for the chance to tackle this task, and to Richard Taub and Katherine Karvunis for making my arrangements at the university so salubrious. I also spent a few very valuable early days at the Program on Non-Profit Organizations at Yale University; John Simon and Paul DiMaggio were helpful then and have been since. I think I will ask the members of the board of the Wieboldt Foundation, past and present, and Jean Rudd, executive director of the Woods Charitable Fund, to stand up for all the foundation board and staff people who have been friends, shared experiences, invented new insights, and shown what a rewarding experience foundation work can be if you push yourself a little and make things go. Jim Joseph, Marj Benton, Pablo Eisenberg, Harold Fleming, and Dick Magat have been especially helpful to this book at crucial moments, and I—along with so many others—have Paul Ylvisaker to thank for giving me my opportunity to grow in this field in the first place.

I've learned from many fine teachers about community; Cecil Butler, Don Leaming-Elmer, Greg Galluzzo, Diane Glenn, Mary Gonzales, Stan and Anne Hallett, Sophia Bracy Harris, Bob Katz, Bob Lynn, Peter Martinez, John McKnight, Shel Trapp, and George Todd are just a beginning. David Greenstone and Barry Karl of the University of Chicago faculty, and Elliot and Frances Lehman of the New Prospect Foundation join several of the above in being totally unresponsible for the final product but important in their reading and commenting on parts of the manuscript. My thanks to Seven Locks Press—Calvin Kytle, James McGrath Morris, Andy Rice, and especially my gifted editor, Jane Gold. They have published some good books and I feel fortunate in having *The First Charity* join the list. I'm grateful to my wife, Diane, who has been patient and frequently helpful with friendly challenges that sweep over me and my Kaypro like a freshwater wave.

Chapter 8 is an edited and expanded version of an article originally published in the May/June 1984 issue of *Foundation News*. The part of chapter 7 about altruism appeared as an article in *Foundation News* in 1988.

Foreword

After a long void in which few important books on philanthropy have emerged, a new generation of publications on this sector of American life has been rushed into print. Some purport to provide new insights into the tradition of giving while others offer new data on who gives and to what.

This book, by an experienced professional in grantmaking, goes beyond the data collection and romanticizing of American uniqueness to offer what appears, at first glance, to be a novel argument: the idea that democracy needs to become philanthropy's first charity. But the use of philanthropy to encourage citizens to become full participants in the public life of their communities extends as far back as early Egyptian, Roman, and Greek societies. Even the creation of the modern foundation stems from the idea that a good society depends as much on the goodness of individuals—the many acts of goodwill that make our society more humane—as it does on the soundness of government and the fairness of laws. Thus, what may first appear to be novel, even radical, is rather orthodox.

But Bob Johnson is no shrill patriot waving the flag on the sidelines of the big event. His grass-roots orientation to community organizations and citizen participation injects a note of realism to a discourse about the effective approaches philanthropy can make to community organizations that often celebrates pluralism while remaining isolated from the travails of those who don't benefit from it. Through well-presented case histories, he challenges us to consider both the enduring roots of our tradition and the many new opportunities for effective philanthropy.

I am particularly struck by his concern with small and medium-size foundations, as well as with family and individual giving. My own experience in this regard is worth recalling. The donors with whom I worked in the late sixties and early seventies took the idea of citizen empowerment very seriously. They operated on the assumption that people whose lives were affected by our funding priorities should be part of the process of helping us arrive at those priorities. We also found that effective grantmaking in support of community development did not always involve highly exciting, "sexy" projects. Some groups simply needed general support money—anathema to many grantmakers but absolutely essential for survival of the groups that must do the groundwork that leads to the glamorous projects many grantmakers covet.

Looking back today, I find that although many of the community projects we supported died a natural death, the people who led them have often gone on to do great things for their communities. They can be found on city councils, in state legislatures, and in other areas of public life where the issues of the day take on flesh and blood. In truth, the potential for leadership was in every neighborhood and almost every organization we funded; but it often had to be cultivated, and individuals had to be encouraged. It was like the analogy of the statue that had been inside the block of granite all along: the sculptor just chipped away the excess stone and let it out. As *The First Charity* suggests, private philanthropy is uniquely prepared to play that role.

The uniqueness of philanthropy lies in its ability to provide for bold action—that special quality that enables a group of private citizens to reform some institutions, to start new ones, and to close out others. But what constitutes bold action is often in the eye of the beholder. Our challenge, both now and in the future, is to ensure the maximum return on every philanthropic investment, and to improve the craft of grantmaking without losing the special qualities of humaneness, spontaneity, and flexibility that have been the genius of private giving in American society.

While the original Greek word for philanthropy literally means love of humankind, organized philanthropy has become more than simply a private act of compassion. Ensuring maximum return on the philanthropic dollar increasingly requires not only private compassion but also a special competence in analyzing needs, meeting the requirements of law, and making certain that every scarce dollar is used for the maximum social good.

Although Americans have always cherished the spontaneous amateur quality of charitable giving, there is a sense in which the complex social needs of our time have made us all professionals together. Thus, the act of charity can be greatly enhanced by both the permanent wisdom and the transitory insights of those who have made the giving away of money their primary calling.

In *The First Charity*, Bob Johnson provides insights that should be of interest to all those concerned about effective philanthropy: donors, trustees of philanthropic institutions, staffs of philanthropic organizations, and the many unsung volunteers who make democracy work by making the ideals of democracy real.

James A. Joseph
President
Council on Foundations

INTRODUCTION

Our well-wishing *can be unlimited,*
since in it we need to do nothing.
But doing good *is harder....*
—Immanuel Kant, 1797

Dr. Kant, as far as giving away money is concerned, it seems even harder to do good now than it was back in your time. Some of the old ways aren't so surefire as they used to be. There is a bewildering array of new causes seeking support. The role of private funds versus government funds is puzzling. So is the increasingly blurry division between some not-for-profit and for-profit enterprises. Too few of the requests we get seem to offer enough promise in addressing the most critical needs and opportunities of our society. It seems to be the right time to think about some different approaches, and this book offers an example of doing that.

"Philanthropy" often sounds like something associated with just the biggest foundations or the gifts of a few vastly wealthy men long ago. I'm more interested in the other side—the families, churches, companies, civic groups, and medium-size and small foundations across the country today that try to be useful in their communities. This book is for people who either are now wrestling with the potentials of these valuable funding sources or may be doing so in the near future. A significant number of new contributors are coming along in the United States; those of us who have been around awhile need to look to them for some refreshing new beginnings and give them the benefit of whatever insights we may have learned along the way.

This book is about what philanthropy can do for American democracy. We seem to have gone about as far as we can go in trying to practice democracy in this country in the twentieth century without becoming more intentional about it. By "intentional" I don't mean a lot of arbitrary policies handed down from high places; political proclamations and expert attention aren't solving the intractable problems among us.

Quite the contrary, democracy needs to become a citizens' enterprise. We need to build a competent public life among us so that an increasingly concerned, knowledgeable, and active citizenry can find answers and pursue them from the inside out. That activity starts not in national circles of government and remote institutions, but in the communities in which we live. No matter how much we may recognize the modern influences of television and everything else that make us less provincial than we used to be, our communities are still the first settings for citizenship for most of us and our families.

There has been much talk about community in the past twenty-five years. There has even been, supposedly, a "neighborhood movement." But darn few neighborhood people have been involved. Too much of the tone has been professional, entrepreneurial— people speaking for others. Too many so-called community organizations have become too far removed from the issues that affect everyday life in communities. The movement has frequently looked more like a reflection of the problem than the path to a solution.

Meanwhile, many of us have moved in the opposite direction from the visions of the neighborhood movement, straying away from feelings of confident community togetherness and grass-roots initiative. Greg Galluzzo, a community organizer in Chicago, addresses the three kinds of alienation he has encountered among us: (1) our alienation from the big systems of government, employment, schools, and other institutions over which we feel we have so little control; (2) our alienation from each other because the internal resources and customs of our communities don't give us as many positive, natural relationships as they once did; and (3) our alienation from our own potentialities because too often we don't feel qualified to join in solving problems and meeting the needs we share with others. Galluzzo offers community organizing as the way to overcome these alienations and strengthen our capacities to determine what we're going to get from our society for education, for job opportunities, for justice, for support when we need it, for a clean and friendly environment, and for everything else that is important to the quality of our lives. Becoming active in a community organization turns out to be not just carrying out good works for the benefit of the community, but taking care of our own self-interests as well.

So the key objective is participation: encouraging ourselves to become effective participants in our democracy, meeting needs and issues directly as communities, finding the best candidates for representative government, voting, holding elected officials accountable, seeking ways to persuade public and private institutions to act in our best interests, and learning through all these experiences what responsible, rewarding citizenship means and where its energies can best be directed.

Philanthropy can't take on each one of us individually and lead us away from our alienations. Nor, fortunately, can it choose our representatives for us, make decisions for us about government, or set public policies. But there is one role for democracy that philanthropy can fulfill: the funding of those community arrangements that seem most likely to help people get together to find answers and make democracy work, specifically in communities where people don't have the means to fund these arrangements by themselves. That's a particularly appropriate role for contributors who have a community base, who want to be a useful resource in local areas with which they feel identified. It's a role that needs to be adopted by diverse independent resources; neither government nor single major concentrations of private power should have a lock on the task of encouraging democracy.

This book is for people who want to take a look at pursuing such a role in philanthropy. It's for people who really want to make a difference with their giving. Without that frame of mind, philanthropy can be a dull and disappointing experience. With it, philanthropy is enriching and exciting work.

Most statements about philanthropic giving are exhortations; we all get tired of the rhetoric and need something more substantial. Philanthropy doesn't have much of a body of knowledge of its own, but there is a great deal going on around us in the social sciences that has important implications for the practice of giving, and I have borrowed from some of that material. What you have before you isn't very long or complicated, but it does ask you to go to school a little. Part One sets out the five promises we expect to have fulfilled by our participation in American democracy and compares those promises with a picture drawn by social scientists of what we actually get in our public life today. It then gives some specifications for new programs, suggests community organizations as a way to meet those specifications, and describes three present examples of effective community organizations. Part Two is about philanthropy's response—the history of our giving habits, our experiences with politics, our chances to be real altruists getting satisfaction from doing good—and offers some comments on the work of professionals, some opinions about what's needed in the field, and some how-to information.

What to call us all is always difficult. *Philanthropists* and the unfortunate *philanthropoids* sound like people giving very large amounts to big institutions. *Donors* has a dolorous tone. So I've taken the easy way out; I keep switching back and forth among these terms and *contributors*, *givers*, *funding sources*, *grantmakers*, whatever. One chapter uses *foundations* fairly consistently. I hope you will find that, no matter what the name, most of what this book says applies to everyone in the field.

Democracy has not been philanthropy's first charity, and it deserves to be. Right now, it's way down on the list. I hope what's here proves useful to a distinguished group of people who want to help change that situation. Such readers have a fascinating, significant opportunity to fulfill a role urgently needed. Our purpose is to live up to John Dewey's ringing expectations:

> I for one do not believe that Americans living in the traditions of Jefferson and Lincoln will weaken and give up without a whole-hearted effort to make democracy a reality.

R. M. Johnson

PART ONE:

THE CASE FOR COMMUNITY ORGANIZATIONS

CHAPTER 1

THE PROMISE OF PARTICIPATION

Warming up to his campaign for the presidency in 1799, Thomas Jefferson talked about the "Spirit of '76." It was fitting that he be the one to coin the phrase. He had been personally responsible for the way the Declaration of Independence defined the spirit of this country, and now, twenty-three years later, he was calling up that document to remind this young nation's citizens of the vitality that was always available, always ready to be realized.

What was—what is—the Spirit of '76? Reading the extraordinary first three hundred words of the Declaration of Independence and looking for the key to their vigor, I'm impressed with how active the language is in speaking from the "people." This is truly a citizens' declaration. Nowhere does it suggest that certain leaders or representatives will do what's best for everyone. Nowhere are there concepts expressed indirectly, telling us that something will get done somehow without saying by whom. It is always the *people* who will "dissolve the Political Bands which have connected them with another [people]," who will "assume among the Powers of the Earth, the separate and equal Station to which the Laws of Nature and of Nature's God entitle them." It is the people who have unalienable rights, who pursue happiness, who give government its just powers, who abolish old government and institute new.

The Declaration of Independence presumes that we will participate in the public life of this country; no one can take charge for us. That is the only way the idea can work. Thus, the Spirit of '76 puts participation at the very core of American democracy. It is the central quality with which we thrive, and without which we lose all we hold dear.

It is also a quality of democracy particularly appropriate to the interests of private philanthropy. Participation is a private experience in freedom and choice for each citizen. Its processes and even its promotion need to be independent from government control. Furthermore, supporting participation is nonpartisan; by encouraging it, philanthropy can enhance our democratic processes without having to take responsibility for espousing specific political views. That needn't be all that philanthropy does in public affairs, but it is an especially suitable primary role because it affirms our charge as citizens to reach our own judgments and act upon them. When private philanthropy does that, it is at its public best.

Participation is not a given. We have to work at it and, if we are expected to do so, there must be some benefits we see for ourselves. We seem to ask that participation do five great things for us:

(1) *Protect us from tyranny.* At the roots of our convictions, the first incentive for citizens participating in decisions about government has always been that doing so will protect us from those in positions of power who would otherwise oppress and exploit us. We know we must constantly work together to prevent tyranny.

The lessons of European history were clear to Jefferson. From Paris he wrote that the people of France were "loaded with misery by kings, nobles and priests." He contrasted what he saw in Europe with the way he felt things should be here: "Every government degenerates when trusted to the rulers of the people alone." For their own safety, citizens must create their government and hold it accountable: "I know of no safe depository of the ultimate powers of the society but the people themselves."

We have a Bill of Rights that shows our distaste for the most dreadful crimes of government, but without an active citizenry our rights will not be realized. The prevention of tyranny becomes at once the first benefit and the first responsibility of democratic participation.

(2) *Reconcile our private individual concerns with public community concerns.* We expect that a citizen's private life and public participation will be mutually supportive rather than conflicting.

John Winthrop, in 1630, talked to his company on board the *Arbella* as it sailed from England to Massachusetts:

> We must delight in each other, make each other's condi-
> tion our own, rejoice together, mourn together, labor and
> suffer together, always having before our eyes our Com-
> mission and Community in the work. . . .

That was a nice balance, valuing both the individualism of "each
other" and the essential collective strength of the community.
Achieving that balance, finding the connections between public and
private enterprise, became a prime ambition of colonial communities. When the United States was born 150 years later, those connections appeared strong and clear as part of the foundation for
our democracy. When Thomas Jefferson's nephew, Peter Carr, was
about to graduate from college, Jefferson wrote him a letter full
of assurance about how the private and public opportunities of
Peter's future were going to complement one another:

> When your mind shall be well improved with science, noth-
> ing will be necessary to place you in the highest points
> of view but to pursue the interests of your country, the in-
> terests of your friends, and your own interests also, with
> the purest integrity, the most chaste honour.

As historian Daniel Boorstin points out when he quotes this letter,
Jefferson believed that "personal ambition should be a prudent admixture of self-interest and public concern."

That's the compact between private and public activity on which
we base our willingness to participate in a democracy. Those who
conceptualized democracy in America were strong individualists.
What made the proposal for a democratic government attractive
was democracy's genius for respecting and supporting its citizens
as individuals while at the same time catching us up in an essential community life.

At the heart of this private-public compact was a powerful new
motivation in our culture: a rising awareness that ordinary men
and women, not just those in the ruling classes, could have some
control, some leeway within which to improve their own and their
children's quality of life. Although today we may take for granted
the principle that says our society allows us to improve our lot,
in the seventeenth and eighteenth centuries the notion of such initiatives among citizens was radical thinking indeed. Further, it sug-

gested a process in which private and public considerations were inseparable. Ruling classes had long known that they were better off if they cooperated with one another. Now there was reason for others to discover that it was in their own best interests to join with others in improving the quality of life in their communities.

John Winthrop's passengers were individuals, varied and ambitious, but in some of what had to be done, they would have to work together. Isolated progress was unlikely, "for it is a true rule that particular estates cannot subsist in the ruin of the public"—that is, if the public life doesn't function right, private lives can't, either. Peter Carr's pursuit would be both individual and public, simultaneously; that was the only way opportunities could be realized.

(3) *Invigorate the individual citizen.* Jefferson spent little time, however, talking about the positive affects on the individual of participating in a democratic society. Like his French contemporary Jean-Jacques Rousseau, he saw freedom largely as a negative value: freedom *from* those despotic conditions that had pervaded so much of the world's experience. Not only did this "freedom from" seem promise enough for democracy, but it also marked the limits of eighteenth-century thinking about the human personality. Given the opportunities of the New World, one could be ambitious and work hard and live up to a certain preordained potential, but there was little recognition of how one's environment and life experience could add new strengths. As John Dewey explains, in Jefferson's time an individual's personality was assumed to be "ready-made, already processed," needing only to be informed by scholarly education and then set free to perform within its given limitations. "It was not conceived of," Dewey continues, "as a moving thing, something that is attained by continuous growth" and nourished, as Dewey believed, by one's public community life.

That's ironic, because the lives of Jefferson and his contemporaries give us our first examples of citizens who themselves gained excitement, insight, and enrichment through their participation in the public life of American democracy. One gets hints of what that life meant to Jefferson through some of the figures of speech he used. There is the example cited earlier, the "Spirit of '76." He liked to call our politics the "boisterous sea of liberty." He referred to the "turbulence" of democracy, which "nourishes a general attention to public affairs." But for him and others it was largely an unarticulated enthusiasm and would remain so until late in the 1800s, when the study of psychology and the social sciences began to give us ways to think about what citizens gain by participating.

The difference of a hundred years is vividly shown in a comparison between Jefferson's and Dewey's perceptions about the relationship between public life and education. Jefferson's conception of education was the teacher telling people what they needed to know. He repeatedly talked about his hopes for education to improve the workings of democracy. If citizens were "not enlightened enough to exercise their control with a wholesome discretion, the remedy is not to take it from them, but to inform their discretion by education."

By the end of the 1800s, Dewey was able to turn this relationship upside down. A nation engaged in the practice of democracy became not just an aim of education but also the setting where education happens. "I believe that all education proceeds by the participation of the individual in the social consciousness of the race" is the resounding opening sentence of the landmark Pedagogic Creed he wrote in 1897.

Dewey's convictions about the importance of learning-by-doing for the individual in a democratic society remained central to his philosophy as it developed over the next fifty years. There are many expressions of the theme in his later works; in 1927 he wrote, "Democracy is a name for a life of free and enriching communion." Participation is expected to be essential not just for good government, but also for the realization of human potentials.

In this process of being citizens responsible for our government, then, we become clearer about our own needs and values, and we learn how they compare with other people's. Some of these other people are in many ways quite different from ourselves. We wrestle with issues that come out of our lives and theirs. We refine some of our attitudes about what's right, what's wrong, what's important, what's trivial, what's familiar, what's strange. We learn to appreciate our own and other people's knowledge and inventiveness. We express our conclusions, we learn to accept the will of the majority when we have been part of the process, and we earn self-respect and dignity by being active citizens. The benefits to us individually and to the community are all of a piece. We learn from the experience, and we feed part of that enrichment back into the democratic political system. It becomes a virtuous circle, a constant regeneration without which democracy languishes and deteriorates.

(4) *Include everyone in our public life.* Jefferson's famous correction to the first draft of the Declaration of Independence, when he changed our most tangible entitlement from "property" to "the pursuit of happiness," was an initial American move toward inclusiveness. He said that to do otherwise would be to "set as zeroes all individuals not having lands, which are the greater number in any society of long standing."

Eleven years later, the writers of our Constitution began its preamble with "We the People of the United States. . . ." Although there was contention at the time as to whom that included, we have given increasing substance to the principle it suggests in the years since. Voting is not all of participation, but without it other activities mean little. Our history shows that we have persistently used our participation to enlarge our electorate toward the universe of the adult population.

The Fourteenth and Fifteenth amendments after the Civil War established the policy if not necessarily the practice of enfranchising those who had been slaves. Several state constitutions in the late 1800s and early 1900s and then the Nineteenth Amendment in 1920 brought women into the electorate; the Twenty-fourth Amendment in 1964 prohibited poll taxes in federal elections; and the Twenty-sixth Amendment in 1971 extended the electorate to include 18- to 20-year-olds. Just as important as these constitutional amendments have been the civil rights legislation enacted by Congress culminating in the Voting Rights Act of 1965, and a wide variety of voter registration activities that today are introducing many citizens to an entry-level experience of participation for the first time. Thus, through amendments to the Constitution, laws, movements, and public campaigns, Americans have affirmed their conviction that participation in a healthy democracy doesn't diminish over time; rather, it expands, bringing more and more of its people into its public life.

(5) *Ensure a safe and satisfying representative government.* Neither Jefferson nor Rousseau were enthusiastic about citizens participating through elected representatives. They placed the highest value on direct democracy, in which everyone participates in decision-making assemblies. The town meeting is our familiar model. But Jefferson recognized the practical necessity for representative government; he grudgingly said it deserved "the second grade of purity."

The danger, of course, was that in any move away from the autonomy of citizens participating directly in decision making, there was a loss of citizens' immediate control, a potential slip backward toward conferring power that would not be held accountable, power that would corrupt. The best safeguard was participation itself. Provisions were needed to help citizens hold representatives accountable and restrict their opportunities for mischief.

The Constitution and its amendments have many such provisions. The two-year tenure of members of the House of Representatives makes for a short tether and prompt accountability. Giving the state legislatures as well as Congress the ability to initiate proposals to amend the Constitution was a deliberate move adopted, according to constitutional scholar Philip Kurland, "from fear of the reticence of the national legislature to correct its own abuses." Jefferson led the writing of our Bill of Rights, three months after the Constitutional Convention. These amendments clearly are aimed at safeguarding citizens from oppression by those we elect. The First Amendment is devoted to this precaution; in it Congress is explicitly forbidden to make any "law respecting an establishment of religion, or prohibiting the free exercise thereof; or abridging the freedom of speech, or of the press; or the right of the people peaceably to assemble, and to petition the Government for a redress of grievances."

These provisions largely reflect a negative approach to ensuring proper representation because protection from abuses was the paramount consideration. In practice there has always been attention to the positive nature of the relationship between citizen and elected representative, and—despite our cynicism—success happens often enough to show the process can be effective. Representatives take to their legislatures the intelligence of their communities, and they bring back to their constituents intelligence about other communities and about issues and options. That process between the people and their elected representatives requires a setting where the relationships can happen, and we look to participation in public life to provide that setting.

These, then, are the promises of participation—five ways in which we expect our public life to benefit us. Is it doing so? Can it do so? It seems useful to look at a contemporary portrait of our public behavior and then see if our expectations are being realized.

CHAPTER 2

THE PREVAILING SPELL
OF PLURALISM

How well is the promise of participation being realized? Are we getting the benefits expected?

To answer such questions, we need to describe today's American public life and then see how the five expectations of participation are faring. The most appropriate description seems to be the interpretation of our public life that behavioral social scientists began to put together soon after World War II. It's a remarkable picture—rich, colorful, full of life—unlike anything we ever had before, based on a great deal of research accomplished with new postwar techniques and technologies.

Social scientists call this interpretation "pluralism." But they don't mean what we usually think of when we speak of our "pluralistic society"—that is, how different we are, yet how well we tolerate one another. In fact, they end up conveying quite a contrary impression because their interpretation emphasizes all the restraints we feel we must place on ourselves to coexist.

The first useful way to look at pluralism is to consider it an objective portrait by experts of how we behave, how we try to get things done for ourselves, how we accommodate to conflict, and how we try to avoid troubles and issues that seem too uncomfortable to address. If you find it ultimately an unattractive portrait, fine; you thereby pass a test that some of the social scientists may have failed. This book is about how we can improve some of our arrangements and earn a better-looking picture of ourselves.

Pluralism, in the experts' portrait, is a style of public life that aims for and achieves an equilibrium among a rich diversity of interest groups. According to this description, day after day, year after year, a free society provides an arena for competition and

bargaining among these interest groups. Businesses and their associations, government agencies, independent public interest agencies, universities, military interests, unions, teachers, doctors, lawyers, other professional people, police, firemen, other public service
workers, transportation carriers, developers, farmers, religious
denominations, ethnic groups, cultural leaders, media, consumers,
property owners, tenants, sportsmen, environmentalists, handi-
capped people, parents, women, men, old people and young
people—all these and many more qualify as interest groups, sometimes local, sometimes national, sometimes international.

In the pluralist arena, every contest for resources, every scrim-
mage for advantage in public policy, is an important game for the
particular institutions and people participating. Consequences can
seem to be momentous victories for some and disastrous losses
for others. But the true aftereffects tend to be modest in terms of
any real shifts in resources and advantages. So that we can resolve
differences and yet not ruin people, we have developed the pluralist
process to the point where it virtually guarantees that the contest
and risks will be limited. Most of the issues involved are practical, short-term working questions; all attention is focused on the
existing situation, leaving little room for theorizing about basic
values, underlying causes, and alternatives that might open the contest up to unpredictably serious consequences. Even when more
ideological subjects get pushed successfully from the world of ideas
and convictions into the pluralist arena, they get reduced to sim-
pler specifics that become proxies for larger, more personal issues.
Busing school children, for instance, has long been such a proxy
in the field of race relations.

Clearly, most of us hope there is enough of this defusing process
and enough screening out of the more troublesome issues to ensure that we will all survive for another day. The pluralist arena
lets us express some of our anxieties and animosities while its constraints prevent those anxieties and animosities from getting out
of control. Compromises cut losses and spread benefits. Losses
are seldom so devastating as to destroy. And for those who do lose
in a given experience, there can be a sense that their time will come
next time, or that it came the time before. Both within each event
and among the continuous flow of events, then, pluralism shows
strong determinants of moderation, limited incremental change,

and a suggestion of fairness. Things even out over time.

Thus, there may be shortcomings, but the fruit of the process is the stability we have enjoyed in this country. The exercises of pluralism become a habit with which we are comfortable, and habit, said William James, "is the enormous fly-wheel of society, its most precious conservative influence."

Robert A. Dahl, Sterling professor of political science at Yale, has been an especially articulate delineator of community life from a pluralist perspective. In his famous 1961 book, *Who Governs?* he describes what makes the city of New Haven, Conn., run as a "system dominated by many different sets of leaders, each having access to a different combination of political resources." Every issue brings out its own set of institutions and people who have their various interests to pursue. All players use whatever political resources they have access to that are appropriate to the occasion. The winners are those who combine, on that particular occasion, the strongest political resources and the skills to use them effectively.

Dahl never claims that the system is totally fair in any idealistic sense. In fact, he provides details about how inequitably political resources are distributed. But he points out that nearly everybody has available some political resources to work with, and that such resources are sometimes used in full strength, sometimes not at all. Often groups with considerable power, such as business leaders and others in his category of "Notables," don't use that power because, in the instance at hand, they don't have that much at stake in the issues. So, Dahl says, there is little consistent domination, and virtually everyone has a chance to win at one time or another. Leaders of the various groups involved express their views, so everyone can hear the alternatives. The system is stable, avoids a lot more serious conflict, is supported by those who generally have the most resources, and usually appears to be acceptable to the rest of the citizens.

As far as participation itself is concerned, pluralism implies that most of us are content to let those out front representing interest groups contend with one another, without becoming too involved ourselves. Some of us participate when an interest group we like is lobbying or campaigning, but such participation is spasmodic at best. Some of us participate more than others. Dahl's study and others show that lower-income people participate least of all. Most interest groups are irrelevant to poor people, who don't have enough resources to start their own, much less any enthusiasm about whether it would do any good if they did.

From the pluralist perspective, there is little or no incentive to promote more participation; indeed, rapid expansion of citizen participation would jeopardize the stability the process gives us. Increases in participation should happen only under control, within the interest group structure, whenever new people can become a force strong enough to join the others effectively in the bargaining arena. Invitations to outsiders to try are rarely given because if they failed to win anything, their frustration would be hazardous to society.

As with other portraits, we can enrich our appreciation of the pluralist description of our society by looking at it in the context in which it was drawn. If pluralism seems a serene picture of a self-satisfied society, that's partly because of when that portrait was originally composed. The two decades following World War II were a time of prosperity for most Americans. Such prosperity made it easy for them to look back through history and see the long-term liberal progress this nation was destined to enjoy. Those less fortunate among us who had little or no reason to feel they were sharing in that destiny appeared to be reconciled to their position. There was little expression of resentment. Civil rights activities in the South were a generally acceptable initiative for reforms that seemed to have more to do with the Civil War than with any implications for the future. Optimism, rooted in a belief in inevitable progress, kept the rest of society from being overly concerned about the poor and those discriminated against. The pie was big and getting bigger so that even those who might get the smallest slices could expect to live a full American life if they took advantage of their opportunities.

It was also a time to reaffirm Americanism. The rise of Nazi Germany from the democratic promise of the Weimar Republic gave us a clear view of totalitarianism and of how it could happen swiftly if one were not vigilant. World War II became a time of virtually unanimous American military patriotism hard for many citizens to conceive of today. It kindled new appreciation for what we have in this country. It felt good to celebrate our convictions that America has a system that works.

The exception to all the good news, however, was the threat of communism, which became a principal object of national concern in the 1950s. Stalin and the Soviet Union became the wickedness to rage against. The fear that Soviet agents and sympathizers worked among us was strong, and it gave new focus to a distrust of those who seemed outside the respectability of conventional American society. It was a good time to sharpen our understanding of what society meant, how it worked, and who belonged, for our own sense of security.

Pluralism as the way we run our public life certainly wasn't unique to post-World War II. But how we felt then and acted made our conduct especially vivid, so that social scientists could capture the essence of pluralism accurately. It was like a photograph taken on an especially bright, clear day.

One motivation involved in the social scientists' portrayal of pluralism needs to be mentioned. Another contemporary description of how America works emerged when Floyd Hunter's book about the centralized, autocratic power structure he saw in Atlanta was published in 1953. It was followed three years later by the strong and provocative rhetoric of C. Wright Mills's famous work, *The Power Elite*:

> What I am asserting is that in this particular epoch a conjunction of historical circumstances has led to the rise of an elite of power; that the men of the circles composing this elite, severally and collectively, now make such key decisions as are made; and that, given the enlargement and the centralization of the means of power now available, the decisions that they make and fail to make carry more consequences for more people than has ever been the case in the world history of mankind.

Both books hammer home relentlessly their authors' convictions that, contrary to any idealistic vision of American democracy, a few overlapping circles of people at the top run the country.

Mills's and Hunter's descriptions of American society received a lot of attention, both inside and outside universities, but many of their peers in the social sciences felt—and still feel—they were oversimplified and unrealistic. Life is more complicated than that, they argue, and there is too little evidence in real life that the grand conspiracies they describe actually exist. Further, the Mills-Hunter view of society is so polarized between those who have power and those who don't that even the most professionally detached political scientist has a difficult time working with this theory without choosing up sides—allying with either the power elite or the revolutionaries. Neither position is comfortable.

Yet the critics agreed that these books and others, including Robert and Helen Lynd's classic *Middletown* studies, were obviously making a valid point about the study and interpretation of how our society works. With the role of government so changed and pervasive, with corporate America and so many other big institutions so influential in our lives, and with international affairs feeling so close to home, the eighteenth- and nineteenth-century concepts of how democracy works in the United States were incomplete at best. There needed to be new descriptions that would recognize the day-to-day interrelationships of business, the military, labor, the church, and all sorts of other groups in the private and public sectors.

So these works of Hunter and Mills and others encouraged social scientists to support alternative approaches. Pluralism became a logical choice—a more neutral point of view that sees a very complex, less ideological design at work.

The new approach appeared to be politically conservative, certainly as compared with *The Power Elite*. Social scientists describing pluralism have been caught up in a trick bag not entirely of their own making. In talking about an important aspect of American society while trying to remain above the battle, they have given the impression, rightly or wrongly, that they harbor no serious objections to the conditions they see. In formulating in pluralism a political design that stresses the value of order and moderation, they have appeared to support our more conservative inclinations. For most of the years we're talking about since World War II, that inclination has been attractive within the institutions and agencies to which the social scientists are attached.

While the behavioral social scientists were completing their portrait of pluralism, dramatic new insights into how we behave in our public lives with one another were coming from an unexpected quarter: economists.

Economists are basically interested in transactions, in how we make choices and carry them out. These choices involve not just money but other commodities—tangible and intangible—available to us as well. When, recently, some especially creative and aggressive economists chose the citizen's power to be engaged in community affairs as a commodity on which to focus attention, they moved virtually overnight into the realm of political scientists, sociologists, and others who fit more comfortably into the fraternity of behavioral social scientists. The new extended family was not and still is not always a happy one because the economists have such different scholarly equipment. Economic disciplines bring new technical means and procedures. A mathematics language becomes germane to the social sciences. So do complex exercises in logic. Models are constructed that show how we may behave when we act *economically*, which means efficiently—investing just what we need to invest to get something we want. That point of view adds some surprising, challenging ways to assess human behavior, many of which lead to conclusions that look very much like pluralism.

The basic economics assertion is that we act out of our own self-interest and then only when the consequences of our individual act of participation look as though they will be worth the effort. In his landmark book, *The Logic of Collective Action*, Mancur Olson explains how we have no reason to join in a public life situation unless two likelihoods are apparent: (1) a particular outcome will be to our advantage, and (2) our own participation will be crucial enough in gaining that outcome to outweigh whatever may be the costs (time, effort, money, risks). Former theories about how groups work maintained that if people are enthusiastic about something they will join in to see that it happens. Olson proposes that such old assumptions fly in the face of logic, and he does so by emphasizing the economic behavior of the individual. If I can assume that lots of other people are going to be involved, my own trivial vote, for instance, isn't going to be significant enough to make it worth the effort to go the polls. If my side wins, I get my share of the benefits anyway. If my side loses, I haven't wasted my time. The chance that my vote will become a tie-breaker is very remote. The more people engage in the collective action, the less likely I am to find a reason to participate, no matter how strongly I believe in what *ought* to happen.

You can shake your finger and moralize at me and ask the fine old question, "What if everyone behaved the way you do?" But that involves a whole different process of guilt, responsibility, and fear of criticism for not participating—complicating factors that aren't likely to be in an economic model. In my own cool, day-to-day economic calculation of what I do or don't need to do to satisfy my personal wants, it's sensible a great deal of the time to say "Let George do it" and not bother. I become, in Olson's term, a free rider.

We have always known and bemoaned the fact that there are a lot of free riders in our society. The difference here is that instead of upbraiding them for being lazy and unpatriotic, the economists' model respects and celebrates the good solid American hard-nosed individualism that their behavior reflects. That shouldn't be the end of the conversation, but it's a useful new part of it. It challenges our traditional American faith in participation. The notion that it can be so reasonable, logical, and "economic" not to join in, not to give, not to vote, is both disturbing and stimulating.

Another smart economic idea about collective behavior is presented by Kenneth Arrow in another highly important book, *Social Choice and Individual Values*. Lots of us have experienced how much trouble a group of people in a car can have deciding on a place to stop for a picnic. Each of us has a different set of criteria about what we're looking for in seeking just the right spot. Individually, all our opinions are perfectly valid and rational, but as a whole among us, they are just an untidy jumble. There doesn't seem to be any fair, democratic way these ideas can add up to a choice that would make sense to the group.

Often the final compromise is a picnic place that doesn't score high on anyone's list of criteria. Everybody grumbles and compares notes and wonders how in the world we ended up in such a terrible place. Perhaps we would have been better off if we had let one person take into account our various prejudices and decide arbitrarily for us.

That homely story describes people confronted with a knotty problem of collective choice, and, again, that's the type of situation that intrigues economists such as Arrow. He doesn't talk about picnics but rather moves ahead to apply the same predicament of choice to the field of electoral politics. He proves with the mathematical disciplines of logic that no matter how rational the individual participants, no voting procedure outside of the most rudimentary polarized situations can be expected to produce results that reflect the sum of our preferences and desires. Quite to the contrary, he and others show a host of ways in which outcomes consistently fail to represent an appropriate "adding up" of the wishes of those voting.

Once upon a time the virtues of the American system might have been described by the notion that we aren't too dependable individually, but somehow we're such good, well-meaning folks down deep that collectively everything turns out pretty much okay at the end of the day. Arrow's economic calculation stands that comforting assumption on its ear. Individually, we may or may not be kind and well-meaning, but at least we can be depended on to behave naturally, rationally, in our own self-interest. The trouble, says Arrow, is when we have to make choices together. It's scientifically impossible to assemble our natural, rational, individual choices into the working order needed for a rational *society*. Thus, we have to invent a more controlled, workable way for our society to make decisions.

There are obvious links between these economic views and the pluralist approach to how our system works. First, Dahl's people in New Haven act out Olson's economic model of participation. They get involved in public life only when there is a clear need to do so to get something specific accomplished, when there is a good chance of success, and when their participation is important to that success and not too costly. Otherwise, they are either free riders or just complete nonparticipants oblivious to what's going on. Second, if, as Arrow says, we can't just naturally make satisfactory group decisions, we need a process that cuts that task down to a size and shape that will work. This probably means that (1) fewer people will be invited to the picnic or at least fewer will be asked to participate in the decision making, and (2) better ground rules for the decision makers will have to be established to free them from having to consider so many different issues and options at the same time.

In our behavior according to the pluralism portrait, we find order in American society by doing just that. We reduce the universe of potential participants down to the economists' rational core— the set of interest groups that have made the economic determination to participate on a given issue. And then those participants simplify their task and ensure social stability by limiting their issues and positions to a clear and manageable agenda. Now the participants are more able to work within the human constraints that both Olson and Arrow describe.

Those individuals principally involved—lobbyists, leaders—have personal career incentives to pursue, promote, and preserve this process. They know how to jockey for appropriate positions, make coalitions, compromise when it's suitable, and back off when necessary. If there is to be a contest, it is understood that the question has to be elementary—only a simple choice between two sides— and that the issues and participants have been narrowed down enough to let everyone involved feel a certain security. They have a clear stake in what happens, but if they lose, they will survive to play again. Then, with everyone lined up on one side or the other, allies are united by a desire to accomplish something specific together despite what may be widely divergent reasons among them for doing so. The contest has become rationally joined. There can be real winners, yet the stakes are low enough to minimize the impact. Our equilibrium is not jeopardized.

The most remarkable feature of the portrait of our public life drawn by social scientists and enhanced by economists is that the system seems to work but we the people become so unattractive. Rationality becomes our only admirable trait, and that doesn't get us very far. In our relationships with one another, we are seen to be selfish, fainthearted, and mediocre. Wimps, perhaps. We don't want to bother with anything that isn't clearly and directly to our advantage, we want above all to be protected from controversy, and it's lucky we have such attitudes because it looks as though we couldn't cope with serious, complicated issues, anyway.

Social scientists have described our limitations thusly:

> There is an enormous mass of evidence. . . [that] seems to demonstrate. . . that a rather large fraction of adults participate in political life barely at all. . . . There is substantial evidence. . . for the existence of considerably less than a widespread and confident commitment to democratic and libertarian norms.

> Individual voters seem unable to satisfy the requirements
> for a democratic system of government.

> In general, people pay much less attention to political events
> and issues than is commonly realized.

> The belief that a very high level of participation is always
> good for democracy is not valid.

These judgments don't come just from peevish theorizing but from extensive behavioralist research. Survey upon survey has shown us to be apathetic, inept, and—the consequent fear of social scientists—dangerously vulnerable if some demagogue were to come along and promise us security and a good time in return for some of our freedom.

The nation's episode with Sen. Joseph McCarthy during 1950–54 left an especially strong impression on social scientists. These were formative years in the development of surveys and polls, and our reactions to McCarthy were probably charted more thoroughly than those during any previous public event. Researchers and observers were able to see clearly how easily the American public tolerated and even embraced concepts that directly contradicted our constitutional principles of individual rights. A Gallup poll in January 1954 showed that slightly more than half of the U.S. population was "favorable" to Senator McCarthy. The percentage stayed above one-third even as the year went by and he was censured by the Senate.

Political scientist David Truman expressed the deep concern he and others have had in reviewing that bizarre American public experience:

> Four years may not ordinarily be a long time in the life
> of a people, but in a time of real crisis it may be just too
> long. In this instance it was very long.

The citizenry had often shown a lack of interest in participating in public affairs. This time, in the view of Truman and many others, there were clues to something worse—our capacities for supporting a demagogue. Among those watching and commenting on the lessons to be learned from our behavior vis-à-vis Senator McCarthy, there were conclusions that ordinary citizens could not be trusted to understand democracy and make it work, and that strong leadership was indeed necessary to safeguard our way of life. The "tyranny of the majority" became an expression full of frustrations about the limitations of our public competence and fears about the weakness of our principles.

Much of the sense one gets in reading the works of social scientists, however, is not of such explicit distrust of the citizenry but rather of just general disappointment with how everything has turned out in this country. Thomas Jefferson could afford to be optimistic with such faith in future generations of citizens; our nation's experience was all still to come. But today we know better. Social scientists and a lot of the rest of us have come to feel that effective democratic participation in the affairs of our nation has not lived up to our—or Jefferson's—expectations, and it's not likely to do so in the foreseeable future.

Albert O. Hirschman looks at disappointment in a way that is close enough in context to be useful here. He cites two inconvenient human traits. First is a familiar psychological phenomenon: we often expect too much from reality. In any human enterprise, at least part of the "hopeful expectations that were entertained were an illusion from the start." Second, along with our affinity for rose-colored glasses, there is our special human capacity to take more risks than other living things. Our expression "trial and error" implies more failures than victories. We are bound (even empowered and privileged) to make more mistakes, even despite any high resolve not to.

Presuming unrealistic rewards in our futures and a propensity for mistakes gives us a double inevitability of disappointment, and in various situations, both privately and publicly, it fills us with a consciousness of expectations gone wrong or unfulfilled. When such disappointment is keenly felt, the likely reaction for a society as well as for an individual is to have a poorer self-image about one's own potentials and to devise ways of getting along that appear safe within those limitations.

It seems possible that the past two or three decades have been such a time of disappointment for many of us in the history of American democracy. We find we have not lived up to our inherited ideals; we are not perfect and the task is tougher than anyone told us it would be. Pluralism is a portrait that reflects a less favorable self-image and lower expectations for ourselves in our public life.

Hirschman gets his interest in the phenomenon of disappointment from seeing how it comes and goes in cycles and how it shifts from one concern to another, and from his conviction that we can learn and benefit by being more aware of these swings. Perhaps if we look closely at the portrait of our public life social scientists have drawn, and recognize what it has to tell us, we can decide it's time now for our American cycle to swing in another direction, to bring our disappointment to bear on what our lower expectations are getting us into, and nudge us along to a new era in which new optimism can be justified.

CHAPTER 3

PLURALISM AND THE PROMISE OF PARTICIPATION

Citizen participation in the public life of this country has been redefined in ways that seem radically different from what we might once have expected. Let's take another look at each of the five expectations of participation and see how they fare under the influence of pluralism.

Protection Against Tyranny

The notion of who has to be protected from whom has been turned upside down. The fox and chickens have had their roles reversed. No longer is the emphasis on extensive, popular participation to keep ourselves free from the development of oppressive, exploitative regimes. In the style of public life described as pluralism, the danger seems to be instability *among* us, a loss of equilibrium if indeed we go *too far* in participation—in numbers or intensity or both.

When we picture ourselves standing in the pluralist arena, we can imagine the inconvenience and disorder that would come down upon us if a relatively large body politic were to object to the way our American democracy functions and decide to use the ballot box or other means to win changes contrary to our traditions. Their actions would certainly upset the prevailing equilibrium. There is also the danger of the inevitable response: should such a movement pose a serious threat, other political forces would feel obliged to move ahead aggressively and establish their own totalitarian control of the society to preserve what they value as the American way of life.

When we dwell on such destructive possibilities, most of us have little choice but to look to those in positions of authority in government as our guardians. We expect *them* to protect *us*.

On a more everyday working level, pluralism also suggests that those interest groups that are active and aggressive need to be protected from one another. Our attitudes within pluralism do keep order, promise benefits eventually for those willing to play, and discourage us from focusing attention on issues that might destabilize us.

To Thomas Jefferson, what we needed to ensure our own security was an active public life among citizens. In society today, we often act as though our best means for protection against trouble is restraint *against* too much public life.

The Private-Public Compact

If Jefferson's nephew Peter Carr were with us today he would sense a distinction between the private and public sides of his pursuit that were not suggested in his uncle's letter to him. As a good eighteenth-century rugged individualist should, he might complain about taxes and regulations, but on the whole he would find freedom and encouragement to use his personal energies as he saw fit in his career in the private sector. In public life, however, he would encounter a different reception. Instead of some sort of broad-based community medium into which he could offer himself wholly and candidly, he would find the array of interest groups. Each group would have its set of polarized positions on specific issues, and Peter would be urged to support those that appeared compatible with his own immediate private interests. But he would find constraints in the options; the scope and the prospects have been narrowed, watered down. In a public life limited to concern about what seem like secondary issues, he would find many important questions inefficiently addressed if at all.

Even our political parties, as described in pluralism, would be less than satisfying to Peter Carr. They are interest groups too, concerned not so much with issues of substance as with the strategic public relations task of finding the political middle ground necessary for winning majorities in our two-party system. Party leadership, like the leadership of other groups, has become managerial and remote. To quote three social scientists who contribute some familiar lines to the pluralist portrait:

> The local party leadership operates at an indirect and unrepresentative remove from the voters. . . . The local party may be an organization for the voters, but it is not of or by them.

> Party government. . . is today at a low ebb in the United States.

> The whole paraphernalia of democratic procedures is employed not so much to insure control from below as to give legitimacy and acceptability to the candidates selected by the leaders.

With interest groups and political parties preoccupied with their own institutional interests, it becomes difficult for Peter and the rest of us to find a context wherein we can write the agenda for our public life in the creative human fashion of which we are very likely capable. That's the most serious consequence of pluralism for us. Democracy needs to have arrangements within which citizens present their felt needs, discuss them, discover their commonality, look at options, reach public as well as private decisions about what's important, and in many different ways identify leadership and hold it accountable. Such arrangements promote a holistic approach to both personal and community troubles, and that approach stands a better chance of overcoming the specified problems without each time generating several others. Biologist Garrett Hardin states the ecological principle: "The world is a seamless web in which we can never do merely one thing." Only with a broad perspective can we begin to anticipate what those other things may be.

But the activity described to us in pluralism limits us to narrow, shallow discussions on yes-or-no questions having to do with a set of specific issues framed by interest groups. Our arrangements cope with such questions efficiently and let us at least temporarily avoid serious trouble. Instead of the hard work, discomfort, and possibility of less controllable arguments that might be in store if we risked broader conversations, pluralism takes such conversations and removes them from reality into a gamelike situation, where we end up in what may be nasty fights but are momentarily safer ones, quarreling about options so isolated they have become abstractions.

To take the example mentioned in chapter 2, when our agenda occasionally entertains what seems a more basic question such as race relations, we find we have cast it in terms such as busing, which let us do no more than live out the meanness that pluralism has told us is our character. But evidently we feel if we can keep the context limited to a token, symptomatic issue, it can remain a narrow dispute, not likely to cause widespread disorder—at least not at the moment.

As behavioralists Bernard Berelson, Paul Lazerfield, and William McPhee say about the process, "It reduces the numerous component decisions (or lack of them) to a single one; it settles the election; and it partially disposes of, without necessarily deciding, many of the issues."

These constraints of pluralism limit the progress promised in our early understanding of the private-public compact, keep us from addressing issues that desperately need public attention, and cut down severely any enthusiasm we might have had for participating in community affairs.

Invigorating the Individual Person

If the pluralist portrait is accurate in showing that we have such limited arrangements for working together to write our public agenda, there is little chance for the personal growth Dewey and others have valued so highly as a characteristic of democratic participation. Most citizens are not engaged at all in those arrangements. The people who from time to time do get involved are limited in what considerations they can bring to the table. The issues have been isolated and simplified; there is little chance to look behind and around the question at hand.

Under such circumstances, it is unrealistic to expect a nourishing public life. There is little learning, little public spirit. The great process described in chapter 1 showed citizens being invigorated by participation and simultaneously feeding some of that vigor back to keep new life flowing in the democratic system. A certain intensity to keep that new life flowing is a good definition of patriotism—a working patriotism, not just rhetoric. Such patriotism cultivates values, builds leadership. It is not likely to happen under the conditions of pluralism described here.

Those who are most troubled by the pluralist portrait focus especially on these limitations. Sheldon Wolin concludes a book entitled *Politics and Vision* with an eloquent paragraph about the need for finding ways in which citizens can bring their whole personalities to public life and work together. When he speaks of "specialized roles" and "separate roles," he is referring to citizens' identification with interest groups. He writes that our task

> is to temper the excesses of pluralism. This means recognizing that the specialized roles assigned the individual, or adopted by him, are not a full substitute for citizenship because citizenship provides what the other roles cannot, namely an integrative experience which brings together the multiple role-activities of the contemporary person and demands that the separate roles be surveyed from a more general point of view. It means, finally, that political theory must once again be viewed as that form of knowledge which deals with what is general and integrative to men, a life of common involvements.

Including Everybody

Pluralism highlights our lack of participation, explains how sensible it is, and affirms that it will be just as well if we keep it that way. As economic, efficient men and women, we join in only when we can see clear personal interests in the outcome and figure that our participation is going to make a difference for us. When we sit on the sidelines, we do the pluralist process a favor because it works better when participation has been reduced to the dependable rational core. "How could a mass democracy work if all the people were deeply involved in politics?" ask Bernard Berelson and his colleagues. Then they add, "Lack of interest by some people is not without its benefits, too."

Another classic position of American democracy, the push toward more and more participation, has thereby been upset. In the pluralist portrait, frequent apathy becomes a patriotic duty—one that most of us seem perfectly willing to fulfill.

To some extent, nonparticipation includes everybody. Dahl describes the way many "Notables" in New Haven are short on political skills and information and avoid public life. They feel they can afford to. They don't need many more decisions in their favor. Individually, they are confident that even when there is an issue of some importance, they can be free riders because there are those in positions of influence who will effectively represent their interests.

Lots of less affluent people stay away, too, with reasoning that is very different but just as logical within pluralism and the economics of collective action. The more modest my socioeconomic position, the less strength I have in any interest group representation, and the less chance I can see for my participation in public life doing me any good.

Nonparticipation thus makes the most sense among the poorest people. They have the least representation in the pluralist contests among interest groups. Compared with their own pressing concerns about basic human needs, they find most of the questions being addressed to be irrelevant. In any economic model of society, where it is transactions that are important, the poor have few of the goods appropriate for exchange. Experiencing their own powerlessness, they have the clearest reasons for deciding that involvement in public life doesn't pay off.

Such exclusion of the poor makes sense not just to the poor themselves but to many of the rest of us. We have begun to use the term *underclass* in the United States. That usage puts us on our way to accepting the existence of a large permanent group of people who live here but don't participate, have nothing to exchange, and don't really belong to the American system. It then has to be acknowledged that such a mass of people will be out of touch with and hostile to the other, participating part of our society, and will thereby be a constant threat to its security. Getting back to the need for protection, the primary function of government then becomes one of protecting the system from this underclass.

More broadly, however, all limitations of participation, no matter what the class, become a self-fulfilling prophecy. No longer do we hold fast to a Jeffersonian ideal of pursuing more and better democratic activity in how decisions are made and the country is run. We are satisfied with something less, and we get less and less.

Effective Participation Through Representatives

Pluralism's emphasis on interest groups shows us that our representatives are not just those we elect. For much of the time, our closer tie to government decision making is through the interest groups that use the many tactics of lobbying, campaigning, giving money, and just being there as potentially strong political forces.

Once more, roles get reversed. Instead of somebody representing us in some sort of lively personal fashion, the interest group itself represents a particular point of view for us. When we support that group, join in its activity, or vote in accordance with its position, *we* are said to represent *the group* and *its* point of view. Instead of the group being our voice, it sometimes seems we are just its troops.

People who manage interest group activities are hardly satisfactory substitutes for elected representatives in leading us into a fulfilling public life. Political scientist David Truman notes how those who run what he calls the "intervening structure"—that is, the interest groups—quickly become limited in their concentration on single issues:

> [M]any leaders in the intervening structure, perhaps especially those whose advancement has been rapid, have gained and held their positions only through an intense specialization, a single-minded concentration on the requirements of power within the group, that hardly encourages awareness of the larger system on which their power and privileges ultimately depend.

As for the impact of pluralism on our elected representatives, we are all familiar with their exclamations about the relentless pressures of interest groups. Their troubles are genuine; interest groups push them hard. The day-to-day demands of their jobs and the opportunities for their future careers depend more on relations with interest groups than on relations with their constituents back home. On our part, much of our contact with our elected representatives comes not directly but through an interest group. When we do get in touch with them directly, it's often because an interest group has urged us to do so; it's only about a single issue and there's small chance for any conversations that help the representatives or us in any broader sense.

How we present ourselves to elected representatives is crucial; we get back what we ask for. If we lead them to believe we are willing and able to consider issues seriously and make responsible decisions, they will know it is in their own best interests to treat us with respect. And under such treatment, we in turn become increasingly competent as constituents. On the other hand, if we lead representatives to believe that we aren't interested, that we are shortsighted, lazy, inept, unable to reach important decisions together, and likely as not to favor crazy ideas and reject good ones, they will feel justified in making more and more policy decisions on their own, dealing only with those strongest of interest groups that press the hardest for certain decisions. When that happens, we as constituents lose both our political competence and the accountability of our representatives to us. To echo Jefferson's words, we then stand ready to be "loaded with misery" by our government. The pluralist portrait shows us drifting in that direction.

So, among all five expectations about participation in American democracy, the prevailing mood described as pluralism severely limits any realization of a healthy public life. The kind of protection we seek discourages participation. Interest group politics work against the development of community initiatives to solve public and private problems. Public life becomes a marketplace for pursuing narrowly defined self-interests rather than a place for learning and growing together. Many of us, especially the poor, get left out. We end up without being represented in government. And as a result, we increase our distances from one another, lose our working patriotism, and jeopardize the Spirit of '76. Equilibrium in society should be a fine objective, but in pluralism it seems a disabling idea, based more on inertia than on the balance of a broad mix of lively energies. As Canadian political scientist C.B. Macpherson says in exasperation, "It is almost incredible. . .that a society whose keyword is enterprise, which certainly sounds active, is in fact based on the assumption that human beings are so inert, so averse to activity."

Little has been said here so far about a special kind of participation: the development of civic leadership, whereby leaders grow in communities and stimulate active responsible participation among others. In the pluralist scheme of public life, there are few opportunities for civic leadership to emerge and prosper. Without career potentials or other clear ulterior motives, the citizen finds no justification for spending time and energy becoming and being a leader. Further, those in charge of interest group organizations are not good prospects for civic leadership since, among other things, they have only their respective thin slices of their constituents' attention. And elected political office, as we have seen, has little potential for cultivating community leadership in our pluralist arrangement.

If they act as this portrait suggests, potential leaders in the more affluent levels of society are apt to follow the lead of Dahl's "Notables" and shun any major role in public life. At the same time, potential leaders in less affluent circumstances are inclined either to lay low or to move up and out of touch with their communities very quickly to positions in which they can be attached to stronger players. In doing the latter, they may provide the country with some respectable examples of upward mobility but they represent negligible leadership in the communities they have come from and in which they may still live.

Without a continuous generation of leadership, without enthusiastic habits of participation in public life, without those conversations that deal "with what is general and integrative," to repeat Wolin's expression, we are most vulnerable to serious trouble among ourselves. Such weaknesses invite the pursuit of other choices—for security or for opportunity—in harsh ways that cause disorder. Equilibrium is supposed to be the centerpiece in the design of pluralism, but the flaws in the design seem to work directly against it.

CHAPTER 4

SPECIFICATIONS
FOR NEW ACTIVITIES

The pluralist description seems accurate enough. Times have changed since it was first drawn, but we have met change with the kinds of accommodation recommended in pluralism.

Many people in this country became less satisfied in the late 1960s and 1970s. Historic movements arose among blacks, Hispanics, and women, and around causes and countercauses concerning the war in Vietnam, the environment, nuclear weapons, nuclear energy, abortion, homosexuality, tax resistance, gun control—all the now-familiar energies of aspiration and protest that were largely unforeseen twenty-five or thirty years ago. Certainly the full potential force of these energies could destroy much of our equilibrium, but it stops short. Movements gain some satisfying victories, suffer some discouraging losses. As they work their way into the pluralist arena, however, their leadership and a great majority of their active constituents are middle-class people, which eases the strain. There may be much heat generated, but in the final analysis there are inhibitions that keep disorder to a minimum.

In the same pluralist fashion, we do indeed choose to avoid confronting basic questions when they seem tough and hazardous. That gets more difficult and bizarre because we must be more aware of such perceived hazards than we were thirty years ago. It's hard to imagine what life could have been like before so many of us found the words and actions to become explicit about discrimination and injustice. It's hard to think of a time when we hardly knew we were using up our natural resources, destroying our environment, or poisoning our water and air. And it's hard to remember the days when we felt more secure against the bomb because we had a few sandbags and bottles of drinking water stored in the basement. Pluralism back then was a convenience and a precaution against obscure disorders; today its protective capacities have become serious business because the troubles are so much more explicit. We have much clearer impressions, from many perspectives, of what it is to be afraid of each other in the United States—not to mention the world.

However, heightened awareness hasn't led to great resolve. Our careful pluralist habits keep us away from major change; we insist that a continuation of our blessed equilibrium will come only from keeping the screws turned down tight with our pluralist restraints, and by doing so we severely limit our chances for overcoming our problems. It is a form of paralysis that John Dewey recognized when he said, "Nothing is blinder than the supposition that we live in a society and world so static that either nothing new will happen or else it will happen because of violence." If social scientists today were composing a slightly updated portrait of pluralism, it would depict a society that too often feels exactly like that.

Interest groups continue to flourish. Most of the available data are about Washington, D.C. Robert H. Salisbury counts more than seven thousand organizations in the early 1980s "in more or less permanent residence" there, engaged in "community of interest representation." He estimates that the number of lawyers in Washington "may well exceed 40,000." He grants that they all aren't engaged in lobbying but figures that those who aren't are balanced by interest group lawyers who come in regularly from out of town.

Then there are the political action committees. Salisbury counts 3,371 of them as of 1983, with most of them representing business interests. According to Sen. David L. Boren (D-Okla.), who is among several in Congress proposing legislation limiting their activity, PACs spent $114 million in support of presidential and congressional candidates in 1984. "Candidates don't have to go back to their grass roots any more to raise money," he says. "They can sit in Washington and get it all from the PACs."

Similar continued growth in interest group activity seems to be taking place on state and local levels. The *Chicago Tribune* reports that there were 643 registered lobbyists working on Illinois state legislators in 1985, double the number six years before. "This spring [1985], special interest groups have congregated here [in Springfield] in record numbers in what lawmakers say is the most intensely lobbied session in memory."

Among the citizenry, however, nonparticipation is still more the norm than participation. The historic movements of the 1960s and 1970s involved only limited numbers of people sporadically. In the 1984 presidential election, only 68.3 percent of the voting-age population was registered, and only 59.9 percent voted. That turnout barely exceeded the one in 1980 only because of higher rates among women, minorities, and voters aged 65 and over; other categories declined. Still, our total performance had improved for the first time since 1964, and we looked forward to a new trend of rising turnout percentages. The 1986 congressional elections, however, showed movement the other way: only 46.0 percent of us voted, down 1.5 percentage points from the 1982 participation rate. In other potential avenues of participation—election campaigning, contacts with legislators, community organization membership, etc.— there are no signs that we have challenged the minimizing traditions of pluralism. The pluralist portrait reflects and reinforces our attitudes. At a time when great questions confront us about money, work, education, natural resources, health, and peace, most of us often decide that we might as well leave such questions alone.

But it's one thing to acknowledge the accuracy of the pluralist description of how our democracy works, and another matter to accept it as the best we can do.

We have some encouragement from the social sciences. After the discouraging research conclusions of the early post–World War II years, more recent studies have given us a better passing grade on the quality of our participation. Contrary to the previous harsh estimates of our competence in elections, "voters seem to be acting more responsibly than had been previously thought." V. O. Key was widely applauded when, reacting specifically to the earlier research findings, he said, "Voters are not fools." When one late 1950s survey was done over again fifteen years later, the researchers "found a substantial increase in ideological awareness among those who vote." Current analysts take us up and down the competence scale but least confirm that the depressing original impressions were not necessarily true for all time.

The civil rights movement has had a recognizable influence on participation. After noting higher rates of general public involvement among those blacks who feel they belong to the movement, one study concludes, "Black Americans have, in group consciousness, a great resource for political involvement." The same study also looks at participation in terms of individuals contacting government offices. It finds that only 20 percent of us have ever pursued our interests in this manner but notes that we seem to know how to do it when we try: "Our data on the content of citizen-initiated contacts shows a citizenry involved with the government in ways that are highly salient to them, on issues that they define, and through channels that seem appropriate."

Where social scientists once accepted pluralism as a desirable or at least an inevitable way for our country to operate, many have grown weary of it, frequently without alternative suggestions. Robert Dahl, on the other hand, stays close to the fundamentals of the original model he helped to describe but wrestles with all the problems he sees in it. Challenged by other social scientists and badgered by his own alarm at our American violence and improprieties, Dahl has persistently broadened the scope of his thinking. With the advantage of being one of the best writers in the field, he has expressed his views well as they have evolved.

Much of his attention has focused on participation. By 1966, he was making explicit his enthusiasm for broader participation in public life—an enthusiasm that had been notably missing from *Who Governs?* five years earlier. In a paper published in the *American Political Science Review*, he answered a charge that he favored low rates of participation:

> I disagree strongly with the notion that high rates of political participation in democratic orders necessarily lead to, or must inevitably be associated with, "instability." I disagree even more strongly with the view that the rates of political participation that have been characteristic of the American citizen body. . .are desirable. On the contrary, I happen to believe that they are deplorably low. I should like to see much higher rates of political activity, particularly among some segments of the population whose participation has been the lowest.

Twelve years later, in 1978, Dahl was carefully dissecting the consequences of pluralism:

In particular, it is pretty widely held that in its effects on decision-making institutions, organizational pluralism. . .often fails to meet reasonable criteria for equality and, partly but not wholly as a result, for a broader "public" or general interest. . . .

[In pluralism,] a stable system can develop in which the most disadvantaged are unorganized or poorly organized and therefore comparatively powerless to remedy their condition. . .; in which major public problems go unsolved because every solution that does not have substantial agreement among all the organizational forces is, in effect, vetoed; in which public policies in every sector are pretty clearly not determined by consideration of what might serve the best interests of the greater number but result instead from the play of organized groups, each concerned exclusively with its own interests; in which, finally, some such perception as this of the way the system operates becomes widely diffused and leads to disillusion and discontent.

And by 1982, he was analyzing "defects," saying that pluralist democracy is "stabilizing political inequalities, . . . deforming civil consciousness, . . . distorting the public agenda, . . . alienating final control [by the citizens]."

As he goes along, Dahl is not pressing toward a design basically different from pluralism. He notes the problems it creates "for which no altogether satisfactory solution seems yet to be found" but then reaffirms his conviction that there is really no other way. Any system, he says, to be democratic, has to "contain many relatively autonomous organizations, including economic enterprises; that is, it would necessarily be organizationally pluralist. . . . Conversely, if it were not organizationally pluralist, I do not think it could be democratic."

It is that focus on the cultivation of a broad variety of "autonomous organizations" that forms the core of Dahl's persistent belief in the virtues of pluralism. After you strip away the distrust and pessimism that our experience with pluralism has produced, that core is available to build upon. John F. Manley has been kind enough to give us the labels "Pluralism I" and "Pluralism II"—

the first referring to the public life described here in chapter 2, the second reflecting a new era when we develop a more constructive style with which to address our community and national affairs. In moving ahead to Pluralism II, we know we are not locked into the impressions of inadequate, incompetent participation characteristic of Pluralism I. The prevailing winds of our citizenship swing widely. We are susceptible to suggestion, either encouragement or discouragement. We have plenty of room within which to work.

For two generations we have underrated our collective interests and abilities in citizenship. It is going to take deliberate steps to change that point of view, promoting new activities that will enhance constructive participation.

What should such activities look like? What will Dahl's autonomous organizations have to do to be effective? For answers, we can turn to the substance of what has been reviewed here so far—the basic essentials of participation and what we know about our present-day experience. From these insights, we should be able to write a set of specifications for programs aimed at improving the quantity and quality of participation, to promote our practice of democracy.

The following is my rendering of such a set of specifications. There are three categories, just to cluster somewhat comparable items: the *results* desired, the *functions* of activities that can be expected to produce such results, and the *strengths* necessary for organizations to carry out these activities.

Results

Programs for participation must

- *Enhance our enthusiasm for public life.* The economic model described in chapter 2 shows we aren't going to get involved unless doing so is clearly attractive to us individually.

- *Enhance our competence in public life.* Being an effective citizen involves specific skills: being able to see what's going on and how it affects you, being able to join with others in figuring out what to do and going ahead and doing it, being able to choose leaders and representatives who are most likely to do more good than harm.

- *Enhance our mutual understanding and respect.* The only way to replace a risky equilibrium based on constraints and fear with a safer equilibrium of positive relationships is to ask that all public activity lead to arrangements where more of us get together constructively. One goal of community public life has to be to realize larger communities without weakening our smaller ones.

- *Stimulate continuous development of leadership in communities.* When an activity generates a flow of new leadership in a community, it shows that it is stimulating more than just token participation among a few people. We need a steady stream of men and women from all types of communities ready to work together in leadership roles without losing touch with where they came from.

- *Promote robust relationships with elected representatives.* We have no alternative but to rely on representative government for much of our public decision making. To make it work, there need to be direct relationships between constituencies and elected representatives that instruct and hold accountable the representative, inform the constituents, and promote open conversation between the two.

- *Be especially effective in poor communities.* Clearly, poor people have fewer resources with which to develop a public life in their own communities and relate that life to others. They are disadvantaged in any pluralist competition. For everybody's security and quality of life, programs to encourage and enable participation need to concentrate especially on effective opportunities in poor communities.

Functions of Activities
To bring such results, new programs in a community must provide

- *An attractive arena for creative discussion in the local community.* This is not the competing, bargaining arena of pluralism but a different, more parochial one involving a significant share of a community's people—a place for community reflection, where needs are expressed, facts brought in, issues identified, ideas invented, and options articulated.

- *A medium for focusing public attention and taking responsibility.* In the arena described just above, the community finds out for itself what's going on and what the options are. It then must choose what needs and issues to focus on, who's to be involved, and who the leaders will be.

- *A medium for effective action and learning in participation.* This is the third leg of the stool. There has to be reflection, then focus, and then an active program and learning from the experience—a continuing cycle of learning and doing.

- *Successes that are both private and public.* Issues and strategies have to be chosen for their potentials to both enhance community life and gain tangible benefits for participating people.

- *Connections with people in other communities.* The experience, at least for many of those involved, has to build relationships with outsiders—allies, representatives of important institutions, fellow citizens.

Strengths Required
To be able to accomplish these things, organizations must

- *Involve significant numbers of people* fairly representative of the communities' population, be governed by them, and encourage broad participation in activities. Organizations must be open and inclusive, and not function like cadres or clubs.

- *Be holistic, integrative,* dealing with as broad a slice of life experience as possible. They must help people see the interconnectedness of different problems and interests.

- *Be independent, autonomous,* not controlled by any single interest inside or outside the community. No instruments of democracy need to be more deliberately community-controlled than programs to encourage and enable participation. Without that quality, they don't qualify.

- *Be in small enough units* to allow people to identify with programs and choose to get involved. The economic model shows us that small groups work better than big groups. Big groups have too many free riders.

- *Have solid, dependable skills in organizing and communications.* Helping people in a community organize their public life and communicate with one another and people outside is a demanding craft. Programs must have solid training components for community people and staff. Leadership has to be constantly refreshed and regenerated to maintain the effectiveness of the program and keep the program representative of the community.

- *Have outside enabling support in poor communities.* Every community has resources, and some of those resources should be invested in community activities. But poor communities don't have enough built-in resources to give people what they need to mount successful programs. They need outside help.

That's a tall order. Certainly there can be a number of different approaches to the task of meeting such specifications. The conviction here is that one option deserves particular attention: the phenomenon of community organizations—independent organizations in local places, governed by residents, dedicated to building participation and leadership and to helping citizens work together to address issues important to them.

This is a field unfamiliar to most and misunderstood by others. The best way to describe such community groups is to give examples. The next chapter presents three community organizations, describes who they are and what they do, and shows how they meet these specifications for effective programs encouraging participation.

CHAPTER 5

BUILD, MOP, and UNO

BUILD, MOP, and UNO are three community organizations working right now in three cities across the country. Stronger than most, they typify qualities of good organizing anywhere. They all share a grand ability to attract and cultivate outstanding community leaders, just a few of whom are quoted here.

Baltimoreans United in Leadership Development (BUILD)

Since 1985 considerable attention has been focused in Baltimore on the pursuit of the "Commonwealth Agreements," a strong new set of commitments for change and progress for Baltimore's public schools. Community groups and school systems in many other cities are watching with interest, "going to school" on the Baltimore experience.

Most attempts to influence big city school systems count on exhortation. We all keep telling the schools what big trouble they're in and urging them to mend their ways and do better or else something terrible will happen. Baltimoreans United in Leadership Development addresses the problem differently, with an approach characteristic of its organizing traditions.

BUILD is a large group of people who belong to churches and community associations that are members of BUILD. They recognize they have no power other than their own numbers and their insights about how things are, how things ought to be, and how things happen. With test scores in the Baltimore school system low and dropout rates high, BUILD's leaders knew from their members that the failure of the public schools was a top community priority. They looked for an approach from which the organization could intervene in school affairs with the best leverage, where the self-interest of the community could be matched to the self-interest of others who had to be involved. They decided that *jobs* were the best first point of entry—jobs students should be able to look forward to and work toward when they're in school; jobs local employers need to fill with dependable, skilled people; jobs the schools need to have in sight for their students to be motivated; and jobs the community needs for its children, so they can contribute constructively to the life, economy, and security of the city.

There was only one way to turn rhetoric into reality. All the key actors involved needed to recognize their stakes in ensuring that more and more Baltimore city children could realistically look forward to decent employment in the area. In a city with critical employment problems especially for inner-city young people, such a positive movement would require serious commitments to special actions.

BUILD began to work closely with Baltimore business leaders through their organization, the Greater Baltimore Committee. BUILD proposed that private industry pledge to make jobs available to Baltimore high schools graduates, and GBC became a working partner in the plan. To date, 114 companies have agreed to give preferential placement to high school youths who win "passports"— that is, those who graduate with an 80 percent grade point average or better and have a 95 percent attendance record.

As those pledges were becoming firm, BUILD and GBC began looking to the school system to join the effort. If the companies were to promise jobs, the schools had to commit themselves to a process of ongoing improvements to produce qualified graduates. The Board of Education agreed to work with BUILD in setting up community committees at each high school. Each committee, composed of parents, teachers, administrators, students, and others interested in school affairs, is expected to see that the passport system works effectively, to draw up its own analysis of what needs to be done to improve the school's performance, and then to pursue the implementation of that analysis.

The members of BUILD, in turn, committed themselves to stay on the case, helping the community committees organize themselves, working with companies to see that they comply with and benefit from their part of the bargain, and keeping the school system's attention on the educational concerns of the plan. Together, BUILD, GBC, and the school system signed a Commonwealth Agreement, pledging to get the work done.

All high schools were not included. As in many other big cities, Baltimore's schools have become a two-tier system, with six high schools designated for citywide enrollment in various academic programs and the other eleven relegated to being "zone schools"—neighborhood schools for the other students. Figuring that the zone high school students needed help the most, BUILD, GBC, and the school administration have focused first on these eleven.

Meanwhile, the second component of the Commonwealth Agreements was being organized. BUILD leadership met with all the private and public colleges and universities in the area. It became apparent that minority enrollment was uncomfortably low and that there was little outreach to city public schools, especially the zone high schools. BUILD worked with each institution on specific packages of financial aid to offer to qualified zone school students—those with passports—who wished to move on to higher education instead of a job. Twelve colleges and universities entered into the second agreement, promising a total of up to $10 million annually in scholarships, loans, and work-study provisions for students with passports. College and university representatives now visit these schools regularly. Also in the works is a standardized financial aid form and a clearinghouse for students at these specific schools, so that if someone is not accepted at one institution, his or her application is forwarded to another.

In spring 1986, parents of 471 students received letters saying that their sons and daughters had qualified for the passports and were eligible for the corporate jobs or higher education opportunities. The letter congratulated the parents as well as the students, saying that it had been their concern and support that had helped their children so much in achieving the standards established by the program. Then the passport holders' names were announced at school. Each Commonwealth Agreements community committee called a special meeting of these students and their parents.

"You'd be surprised at the impact that simple announcement had," says Gary Rodwell, now past president of BUILD. "There was an excitement that spread through every passport holder's household. Each one of them became an overnight role model. They'd look at that letter and say, 'Hey, I got a job!' and suddenly we'd been able to put meaning back into a diploma. People had known about the program, but it wasn't till they saw it really happening that they appreciated it."

In 1987, there were 628 passport holders, a third more than the year before.

As with all grand designs, it's not all as easy as it sounds and there is much to be done. Although the school superintendent is very supportive of the program, not all the high school principals work at it enthusiastically. The level of community involvement varies as well. Top corporate management is ready and willing to make the passports a reality, but word doesn't always get through effectively to personnel departments. Some colleges and universities are indicating that the original understandings about levels of financial aid were not realistic.

Further, in a broad-based community organization such as BUILD with so many parents involved, there is a healthy pressure against letting anybody be satisfied with "creaming"—that is, helping only a small group that happens to score at the top. Six hundred and twenty-eight students in 1987 is still only 12 percent of the graduating classes in all Baltimore high schools. Too many students fail to qualify for passports on the basis of inconsistent and questionable attendance records; and lots of people are saying that high school is too late, that more intervention is needed at the junior high and elementary school levels.

It's up to BUILD to lead the way in addressing these concerns. The community committees of school personnel and neighborhood residents are now being organized; they will be formally constituted and linked together in an association that in turn will become an institutional member of BUILD. New rounds of meetings with companies are being held to develop better loyalty to the program down through the ranks. And corporate personnel representatives are visiting the schools and talking about jobs with current and potential passport holders; in addition to their value to the students, these visits also imbue the visitors with more respect than they may have had before for the capabilities of the students who are gaining passports.

Further, at follow-up conferences with higher education officials, BUILD leaders acknowledged the institutions' problems with their

financial aid capacities, but then they pressed for new, creative solutions to these problems so that all qualified applicants could have
a better chance for a good college education. As far as creaming
is concerned, an alternative passport is being proposed—perhaps
silver instead of gold—for a second category of hardworking students who don't reach the 80 percent grade point average. Special
education students also need to be included somehow; a handi-
capped high school senior with a fourth-grade reading level made
an eloquent speech at a BUILD meeting at which he said he looked
forward to the time when he and others like him will be served
by the agreements. BUILD is asking the superintendent of schools
to look at the attendance record-keeping procedures so that some
students are not unfairly penalized. Finally, the local school committee structure is being designed to expand participation to the
junior high and elementary schools that feed into each zone high
school.

Of the 471 students who won passports in 1986, 60 percent chose
to use them to move on to higher education and 30 percent chose
jobs. The remaining 10 percent did not use their passports, at least
not directly for options available through the Commonwealth Agreements. Of those who chose jobs, only one was not employed within
a reasonable length of time, and only seven were no longer with
their original employer after six months. "The majority of the jobs
are beyond entry level," reports Mr. Rodwell. "There is enough
visibility in the program to keep that percentage up, and we've got
some companies that are beginning to say their experience is so
good they want more city kids."

In looking beyond the usual ineffectual statements of the problems
of big city schools, the Commonwealth Agreements make the course
clearer for everybody. Students can see a real difference in how
the adult community presents itself. Instead of just getting admonitions to stay in school, they are being offered a practical, realistic deal: if they do their part, there's a job or an opportunity to
go to college. That's a dramatic change. Companies now have a
specific promise of quality candidates for the local work force, both
before and after college, and they can look to somebody in
particular—the school system and the local colleges and
universities—to deliver on that promise. The colleges and universities have a built-in selective recruiting process that yields promis-

ing applicants in categories they need. The school system is able to impress its students with a whole new incentive system that directly ties a desirable future gain to the students' performance at school. And by accepting responsibility under the Commonwealth Agreements, the schools have been *authorized* by BUILD, the GBC, and their constituencies to do what's necessary to get the job done and ask for the resources required.

At the center of this activity is BUILD, a nine-year-old citywide community organization made up of forty-eight churches, the Baltimore teachers union, the Baltimore principals and school administrators association, a hospital workers' union, and a new public housing tenants organization. The church members—Catholic and Protestant, 90 percent black—include poor people, working class, middle class, employed, unemployed, underemployed.

BUILD's program differs from other campaigns to reform public education in that (1) it was initiated by a community organization made up largely of lower-income black residents of the city, and (2) it uses the sensible, powerful strategies that come with bright, practical community organizing activity. In appreciating BUILD's success on this issue, it is crucial to understand how the strength of the initiative came not from some new, narrow school reform effort but from the power and experience of a broad-based, multi-issue community organization already in place.

Further, the organization's ability to take such creative leadership in school affairs didn't happen overnight. BUILD had long been looking for ways to tackle school problems. Just recently, it had exposed widespread lack of essential supplies at schools; the new school superintendent's constructive response to that problem encouraged BUILD to propose a much more far-reaching effort. It was through a series of research actions by BUILD members themselves that the organization became especially interested in the Boston Compact, a pioneering effort involving public schools, businesses, and other institutions in Boston. BUILD leaders and staff made three trips to Boston to study the program there and look at the differences that needed to be considered—both because Baltimore isn't Boston and because a second-generation program should learn from the strengths and the weaknesses of the first. It was a fresh interpretation of that concept, made for Baltimore by community people, that became the Commonwealth Agreements.

BUILD had also had experience with the area's corporations. It had been pressing the GBC on issues concerning three job development categories: the unemployed and underemployed, racial discrimination in middle management opportunities, and employment for the next generation. It was this last question that drew the attention of the GBC, and BUILD leaders began talking with them about collaborating on a program for the city's high school students. It has been commonly known that Baltimore-area companies have been hiring more people from outside the city and fewer from Baltimore itself. BUILD expects the Commonwealth Agreements to help reverse that tendency.

So, though the mechanics of the Commonwealth Agreements are interesting indeed, it always has to be remembered that the most ingenious community idea in the world won't work without the power of a large, well-respected, bona fide citizens' organization behind it. BUILD builds its problem-solving capacities from its strengths of participation and leadership.

Essential to the development of BUILD's style and strategies is its relationship with the Industrial Areas Foundation, the center of organizing energy developed by Saul Alinski in the late 1940s. The IAF provides on-going staff direction and extensive training for BUILD. Two hundred lay members and clergy of BUILD churches undertook comprehensive leadership training in Baltimore last year.

Over the past seven years, 130 BUILD leaders have been involved in national IAF training programs, where they meet and engage with leaders and staff from the rest of the richly diverse IAF network, which includes organizations in Texas, Southern California, New York City, and Tennessee as well as Baltimore and another area in Maryland.

What leaders learn most from the training is competence and confidence in organizing for the benefit of their own neighborhood institutions, communities, and themselves. Like other IAF affiliates, BUILD recognizes the necessity of building strength in its member institutions and looks to the leaders within those institutions to help people give effective attention to neighborhood problems. Police protection, garbage pickups, streetlights, arson, rats, abandoned buildings—these issues are addressed by church membership as they are raised in the community. Leaders ask other leaders and the BUILD staff for strategic advice, but the responsibility for such initiatives has to be theirs.

Leaders from individual churches become representatives on a steering committee and ultimately members of the "strategy team." The team is officially the board of directors of the organization, but BUILD avoids the label. As Gerald Taylor, IAF lead organizer at BUILD, says, "Boards of directors are usually staff dominated and aren't in the business of developing people." The strategy team, made up predominately of lay leaders from the congregations, gets proposals for BUILD's citywide work from the churches, individuals, wherever problems and opportunities are identified. The team decides on an agenda, which has to be ratified first by the steering committee and then by the delegates' assembly, where groups from every member church come together. Over twenty-five hundred people attended BUILD's most recent convention.

BUILD's budget for 1987 was $120,000. The organization is lean; overhead and administrative costs are minimal. Half of the budget goes to the IAF for Taylor's salary and IAF training for leaders and staff; half of the balance pays for two organizers in training.

Almost half the income comes from dues paid by each member organization at the rate of $4.00 per adult per year. An ad book nets $40,000, and the Campaign for Human Development of the U.S. Catholic Conference is currently contributing $30,000.

BUILD is a 501(c)3 tax-exempt organization. Some of Baltimore's corporations used to contribute, at least buying ads in the ad book. But when BUILD waged aggressive campaigns against the city's banks for redlining and against the utility company for rate increases, corporations withdrew support. Now, with the Commonwealth Agreements experience, the attitude toward BUILD among corporate Baltimoreans is probably changing. While there is certainly no assurance that future disputes won't occur between BUILD and the city's major public and private institutions, there will likely to be more respect for BUILD's capacities. Present opinion was reflected in newspaper editorials when the agreements were officially announced. Crediting BUILD for its initiative, the *Baltimore News-American* accurately identified the core of the Commonwealth Agreements' vigor in comparing it with previous strategies: "The failure of past efforts to solve [school] problems of achievement, attendance, and job placement is evidence that ignoring the link between school and the workplace has been unwise." And the *Baltimore Sun* said that BUILD "is proving to be an effective vehicle for moving the concerns of the urban poor and middle-income people into the spotlight where they cannot be evaded."

But the most important change generated by BUILD activity is in the attitudes of community people themselves. Participation in BUILD has shown them they *can* make a difference—for their own benefit and for everybody else in Baltimore. Rev. Douglas Miles, pastor of Brown Memorial Baptist Church, sums it up:

> I used to be overwhelmed by the problems of the depressed West Baltimore neighborhood my church serves. The church simply had no resources to serve the poor, and I never envisioned being able to get the ear of the city's corporate and political elite. BUILD has changed all that. We have the confidence and the skills we need to help the community—and the whole city—move ahead.

(The following is from my interviews with Gary D. Rodwell, a member of Union Baptist Church on Druid Hill Avenue in Baltimore and past president of BUILD. He has been active in BUILD for six years.)

What's BUILD's secret of success in putting together
the Commonwealth Agreements?
Mr. Rodwell: Basically the same major ingredient that has gone into all our successes: you depend on good people from the community to see that their own views and those of others are heard. BUILD's name tells it all. We are Baltimoreans united in leadership development.

And then to mobilize people, to galvanize all of us, you have to respect our self-interests and the immediacy of those interests. The schools in our city are of immediate importance for our generation. I don't have children myself, but that doesn't mean I don't know how essential it is for the schools to improve, for me and everybody else. We weren't organized in a way that could help the schools do their job better. Neither were the corporations. None of us were serving our kids the way we were supposed to. We in the community who have to depend on the public schools knew that better than anyone else, so we had to be the ones to start doing something about it, seriously.

What good has the Industrial Areas Foundation done for you?
Mr. Rodwell: The IAF has been around the game for a long time.
They know what it takes. First they help us change our lives; they
tell us we can act on the values we have around our families, our
religious life, and the workplace. They tell us there is a way we
can speak and be heard. We can sit at the table and be part of decision making—not making unreasonable demands, but affirming
that people have a right to justice.

Second, they stick with us. The training programs fuel me, give
me hope. I find there are other people in other cities who have
the same difficulties we have, but they also have their successes
and stories about how their organizations are growing. I get to know
that we aren't just isolated here.

Then many times we've reached crises and would have fallen
into traps—vested interests of some members against others, turf
wars. The IAF helps us survive those internal troubles before they
get hot.

Those are the things we pay them to do. We evaluate them. If
they don't help us build and maintain the organization, we can fire
them.

*How do you avoid having BUILD get top-heavy, with leaders
spending more and more time on big citywide issues and losing
touch with the neighborhoods?*
Mr. Rodwell: When BUILD approaches a church, it tells the people they will get two things from the organization: leadership will
be trained to help the church address its own issues and the problems
of the local community, and people will get individual development and growth as they become involved in the larger organization addressing citywide issues.

It has to be that kind of a double-edged sword to get what you
need. The larger organization is only as strong as the individual
churches. So BUILD isn't built on the issues themselves; issues
are used to foster relationships among us, both in each church and
between churches. At my own Union Baptist Church, we would
never get a chance to touch the lives of some other church like
Guardian Angel Episcopal, which is white. Or them us. When

you're in BUILD, though, you get that chance. You work hard together and when you succeed it's a climax you all celebrate. When you get it all together, it really works.

And remember that with something like the Commonwealth Agreements, it's back at each local school that the agreements are going to either work or not work. We may be negotiating at the citywide level but it's just so we can put the action back where it's supposed to be, in the community around a school.

You make Baltimore sound pretty good. Do you figure you've got it made, or are you worried?
Mr. Rodwell: We're always worried. Baltimore's a strange city. It's really two cities. On one hand it's leading the country in renaissance, in the inner harbor projects, in rebuilding downtown. On the other hand, it has high levels of unemployment, segregation, and high school dropouts.

It can't go on that way, with the majority of the population not getting a commensurate share of the progress. There are going to be people venting their wrath, and a lot of innocent people are going to get hurt, if we can't build structures in the community leading us away from that condition.

BUILD is one of those structures and we take the responsibility seriously. We know that it's up to us to be the watchdog on the Commonwealth Agreements. It's a lot of hard work. We have to beat a big drum, and there never are enough of us to do the beating just right. We get really maxed out in terms of overload on leaders, but we just have to find more. Everybody knows if BUILD doesn't make the system work for kids and families, it's not going to work for them either. If we don't keep pushing for better schools and meaningful, decent jobs for the young people who work hard and get their passports, we'll just be perpetuating the city's problems. BUILD has to keep on representing the values of what's important to people.

Metropolitan Organizations for People (MOP), Denver, Colorado

Vicki Ceja and her family live at the bottom of a hill on the northwest side of Denver. When it rains there's a lot of water and mud slides. She had complained to city hall and her councilman about the mud in the yards and streets, but nothing happened. Then she talked with a community organizer from Metropolitan Organizations for People.

"He said if we could get a group of people together who were also concerned, we could probably get some results," she remembers. "So we got the neighbors together from four or five blocks and had a meeting about what the neighborhood needed. We all agreed on the mud problem, went back to city hall as a community, and eventually got a Community Development grant for sidewalks, curbs, gutters, and a retaining wall to stop the slides. That got us to thinking about what we could accomplish if we organized as a people."

Ms. Ceja and many of her neighbors belong to St. Rose of Lima Church. They and their pastor began a parish development process. "St. Rose became the foundation; the community became the place where we could act out our faith together. If you believe that people have the right to a decent life if they'll work for it, you need a way to get there effectively." The way was building a community organization of their own and affiliating with MOP.

One issue the parish addressed with the likelihood that, in the proposed expansion of an industrial area adjacent to their community, a substantial number of families would lose their homes without even being involved in deliberations about the plan. Although a zoning change was required, minimum notice had been given and, as Ms. Ceja says, a lot of people just assumed they had no rights or chances to stop the development, anyway. But they did want to save their homes.

"So we all went out and learned about what was going on and what we could do about it—especially the people who lived in the area. We talked with everybody involved, we testified, we showed what the community would lose if the change went through.

"We won and the development was blocked. The experience paid off tremendously because neighborhood people led the way and did the work. MOP didn't become some advocacy group doing it for those families. They did it themselves. Now they know they have something to work for. They know they can use their own strengths and resources. They are fixing up their houses, cleaning up the blocks. The place really looks like a neighborhood now.

And outsiders have to look at our whole part of the city differently, as a respectable place where people care."

Vicki Ceja is now president of MOP. Her parish, St. Rose of Lima, is one of twenty-five members of MOP. Twenty-one are churches—ten Catholic and eleven Protestant (Methodist, Lutheran, Presbyterian). The others are neighborhood organizations not attached to a church, or at least not to any one church in particular, in the city and suburbs and out in Adams County to the north and east of Denver. To be a member, a group pays annual dues: $3 per church member for congregations, $1 per member for neighborhood organizations.

Since MOP was organized six years ago, its membership has been largely Hispanic and white. It has occasionally joined with and supported a black community group centered in northeast Denver. With that group becoming less active, however, MOP has talked with black church representatives about developing a MOP-related organization. Twelve churches are coming together to form a sponsoring committee for that purpose.

Sometimes several member organizations will get together around a shared concern. All four MOP member organizations in Adams County have been concentrating their attention recently on the area's water supply because reports of serious carcinogenic contamination have been confirmed by the U.S. Environmental Protection Agency. The groups encouraged the EPA to press its demands for correcting the situation and insisted that the water board and health department commit themselves to a cleanup schedule, an immediate analysis of where the problem was coming from, and a study of how the water was affecting the community's health.

It became clear that the U.S. Army's Rocky Mountain Arsenal was at least one source of the toxicity and that the situation was indeed disastrous with lethal chemicals deeply entrenched and seeping into area wells. With no immediate solution in sight, there followed a period of sensible absurdities. For instance, the health department told the adjacent community of thirty thousand to boil its water indefinitely. After meetings with eight hundred MOP Adams County residents along with congressional representatives and a sometimes reluctant EPA, the Army admitted that the arsenal was a "possible" source, and Army representatives offered to provide bottled water for all school children.

By now there was great community alarm and pressure on the Army to act quickly. Subsequent negotiations produced both a $1 million fund from the Army to bring in a portable temporary filtering system that would work for a year and a $6 million commitment for a more permanent filtration plant that would at least ensure clean water from the wells supplying the present community. Any thoughts of more extensive filtration at other well sites, or of eventually getting to the source of the problem to protect the underground aquifers for the whole region, would have to wait for some enormous government intervention in the future.

This was a heady period for MOP in Adams County. A few leaders experienced a time of what they and others called "super-empowerment," when they suddenly found themselves in a highly visible and influential position on the water supply issue. Such times can make or break a community organization. The few at the top can take their exalted position all too seriously and cut the ties of their accountability to their community groups, leaving both them and their groups much less influential and useful than before. Or they can make a deliberate effort to keep expanding the ranks of the core committee at the top, and provide for extensive reporting and meaningful participation among the increasing constituencies throughout the community as the issue heats up and more and more people want to be involved.

MOP pursued the second route carefully and, by and large, successfully. According to executive director Mike Kromrey, "We just kept making more and more phone calls and having more and more meetings. We all insisted that decisions had to be made in committee, with lots of discussion. Everybody had important roles. With this kind of a decision-making process, no one could move out on their own as some sort of expert. This way leaders were protected from any temptations to cut deals on their own—and, believe me, there were plenty of opportunities."

When one or several MOP members identify a problem that needs to be addressed on a metropolitan- or citywide basis, they meet with other members to solicit their involvement. Then, if enough groups find they have the issue in common, they appeal to all MOP members at the annual convention or at one of the quarterly delegates' assemblies. If a significant number of members agree, the problem becomes the focus of a campaign that involves all MOP member groups wanting to join in. It is made clear, however, that if a group doesn't want to take part in a particular campaign, that's all right, too; protecting the autonomy of the local parishes and neighborhood organizations is of paramount importance.

The first major MOP campaign evolved over a four-year period around concerns about utility rates and regulations and how they are determined. Often working with other organizations, MOP fought successfully for fairer, more modest rate structures, and it won restrictions on the circumstances in which service can be cut off if charges aren't paid. MOP showed strong leadership in the campaign for an Office of Consumer Counsel at the state legislature, an office that now helps consumers, small businesses, and farmers keep track of utility issues and ensure proper representation. With MOP encouragement, both Public Service Company and Mountain Bell endorsed the bill establishing this office. A recent report on the office assessed the record of its activities and found that it had saved consumers a total of $200 million in 1986 by defeating rate increases or winning reductions, and by successfully claiming that there had been overcharges.

Now the major thrust for MOP, mandated by this year's convention, is to organize a Citizens for Better Education campaign. Not just Denver but other communities in the area as well are suffering from high dropout rates and poorly equipped school graduates. There is little history of organizing around school issues here, so MOP is beginning at the most local level. Parents are meeting and identifying concerns and problems of all kinds, from inadequate numbers of textbooks to drugs to poor reading skills to lack of easy parent access. They are choosing some winnable issues and working on them. As they move along, parents—as well as teachers, students, and others—will get together to research what's happening in other cities and decide how they want to approach the more fundamental issues.

Kromrey points out that the Adams County members of MOP who were deeply involved in addressing the water problems are now active in this process as it relates to schools, and he sees that as evidence of good organizing. "We're always talking about how you should be able to transfer the enthusiasm and skills that have been generated in one experience to another issue, and here is a case where that has happened well. We figure that the lastingness, the continuity, is because our strong institutional base in the churches gives the organization so much stability."

Where *campaign* is the term reserved for a joint activity of all or most MOP member organizations, *coalition* is used to signify times when MOP gets together with other organizations on specific projects. In 1984, MOP joined others in a coalition to win a city ordinance on the transportation of hazardous materials through the city. Though the concern was not limited to military materials, a torpedo spill occurred at Denver's major interstate highway intersection soon after the coalition had begun its work, and the news reports helped define the seriousness of the issue. The coalition made a strong case, brought in an expert for the city at the coalition's expense, and got a comprehensive ordinance passed unanimously by the city council in 1985. The new law, regarded as one of the best researched and workable ordinances of its kind, designates certain routes, specifies safety standards, and establishes an inspection and permit process.

MOP members meet a broad range of elected representatives and government and corporate officials in campaigns and accountability sessions. "I've learned how the system works," says Ms. Ceja, "and the strength of people power. We have meetings regularly with our legislators in the neighborhoods. Out in Adams County, one of the MOP groups forced the county commissioners to have the first evening hearing they've ever held. . . . You know, politicians talk about being for people but they have a real hard time staying right there. We elected them, and we figure we've got the best chance to make them work for us."

Ms. Ceja likes the broad variety of people MOP pulls together, with members from St. Rose of Lima and other city neighborhoods alongside the members of Adams County groups. "It adds some spice of life. There were some tensions to work through, but we learn a lot through our differences. We can even see some differences among *them* themselves out there in Adams County. Now they come join our board and the circle opens up to include them. It opens us up."

The checks and balances in authority among the churches, neighborhood organizations, and MOP as a whole is at once the key to MOP's success and also the volatile quality that must always be watched and attended to. Dolores Martinez, former president of MOP, acknowledges that the responsibilities and opportunities as president brought growth and new horizons for her, "but you've always got to keep the basic neighborhood values in mind. It's love of family, justice, peace, honesty that keeps us together. What's the point of having a big complicated structure with a lot of coalitions if there isn't a base?"

Ms. Martinez has become a leader not only in MOP but in other city and state organizations as well. Her insights about leadership are crystal clear:

> You can't let people put you in the position of taking credit by just accepting their thanks and tributes when they say you've done something nice for them and the community. Sometimes that seems like the easiest thing to do. But instead you've got to respond with the truth—that it wouldn't have happened without them being involved and it won't happen again if they don't join in more. . . . It's so easy to become burned out; we always have to be looking for new leaders, keeping our ears to the ground, finding the people others respect, offering support and training.

She was named Hispanic Woman of the Year in Colorado in 1984. But, again, she emphasizes the importance to her of maintaining close ties to the local community with which she identifies. "My new friends are silver plated; my old friends are gold."

Until funding got tight three years ago, there were the staff director and a half dozen organizers, four of whom were provided under a contract with Denver Catholic Community Services. Now there are only Mike Kromrey and two organizers from DCCS. With funding from the Campaign for Human Development, MOP is going to add a black organizer for the new work in the black community. The budget before this addition is $90,000, which they will cover largely with self-generated income from dues, ad books, and fund-raising events, and with support from religious denominations. MOP has a goal of becoming at least 60 percent self-sufficient within three years.

Kromrey talks about what the staff does: "Everybody works on the MOP campaigns when it's necessary, but the first priority all the time is helping the congregations and neighborhood organizations develop themselves, address their own concerns, and build their relations with MOP and the other MOP members. It's not like starting a lot of block clubs, which then sort of 'belong' to you. These are respectable existing institutions in MOP. We have to earn the right to work with them. We do that by providing an environment in which they can engage in (1) reflection, (2) education, and (3) action. What they find they want to do may be anything from organizing on neighborhood issues to mutual aid projects. It's important if it's important to them, like a parish now that wants us to help them start a food co-op."

For help in training both leaders and staff, MOP uses the services of the Organize Training Center of San Francisco. Leaders go to OTC's five-day training programs held twice a year; nine went last year. There are a good many phone calls back and forth, and OTC representatives visit periodically to meet with staff and leaders.

"OTC has been instrumental in what we've been able to do," says Ms. Martinez. "The five-day sessions have given us the nuts and bolts of organizing. Then we asked for a special workshop on conventions before we had our first one, and OTC had us go to another organization's convention as part of that. When we wanted to put out an ad book, they showed us a very successful one from another group.

"Most of all, they know our history; they've been with us through the evolution of our organization. They are great on stress and burnout—how to get through it yourself and how to help others. A while ago they helped in my own parish; we had a controversy and they got us to go to someone here in town who's an expert on conflict resolution.

"They keep asking us over and over again what's important to us, what our values are."

Ms. Martinez's thoughts about MOP's experience with the hazardous materials transportation coalition are interesting. Not many community organizations like MOP become involved in issues of national defense and peace. "But when MOP joined in on this activity," she says, "it made a lot of us more aware of the military around us here and the connections between so much military spending and what we need so desperately in our communities. Working with other organizations in that field opened up some new avenues for people."

Although there is pressure to expand the membership, especially the plan to add a larger black constituency, MOP's board of directors always lists as its first objective the achievement of a core team—at least five to seven leaders, each of whom has a solid "following" of at least five to seven others—within each member institution. That takes a lot of local neighborhood work. The tone is cautious and deliberate. "Organizing like this is new in Denver," explains Ms. Martinez. "It's taking some time for people to have a few victories and feel more confident about tackling community problems."

Ms. Ceja says the same thing: "The most important thing is for people to be able to look at a problem and say, 'Hey, we can do something about that!' "

United Neighborhood Organization of South East Chicago (UNO)

The United Neighborhood Organization of South East Chicago joins together a variety of smaller groups in a seven-square-mile area on the southeast side of Chicago. Membership includes major churches and, to a lesser extent, neighborhood organizations, unions, and social service agencies. Six hundred people representing twenty of these groups in the community attended UNO's fifth annual convention in May 1986. The delegates were 60 percent Hispanic, 20 percent black, and 20 percent white, reflecting the racial proportions of the area.

According to Mary Ellen Montes, a leader who has since been elected UNO's president, "When we build an organization in a neighborhood, people begin to know their neighbors. And I'm talking about a diverse population like South Deering, where I live. It's got public-housing families, older Anglo families still here, Mexican-American and Mexican families, and black families. Organizing to solve problems makes us closer; it's a good feeling.

"Then UNO enlarges the circle. [Referring to three parts of the area] Bush is Bush, Manor is Manor, South Deering is South Deering—we will always have our separate bonds. But UNO gets us to see we all face the same types of problems and we're better off together than we are alone. UNO helps us realize that change is possible."

In preparation for the annual convention last year, the member organizations held special meetings individually to decide what problems and issues UNO should address in the coming year. Then ten or more representatives of each group brought the recommendations to a delegates' assembly, a working session where priorities were determined and slates of candidates for the board were established. The annual convention then discussed and voted on the priorities and elected a board. Action development committees were named to develop specific plans for each area of concern.

The top priority had to be the continuing problem of a disastrous loss of local employment. UNO's area has long been dominated by Chicago's steel mills, adjoining the community along Lake Michigan. Community families have long traditions of steady employment in the mills. In the past several years, however, mills have closed and total production has been drastically cut, resulting in a concentrated unemployment problem that has been crushing for steelworkers, their families, and the community as a whole.

The troubles have been exacerbated by the area's recent population change. Numerous longtime white residents have moved out, and Hispanics and blacks now comprise most of the community's population. Many of the latter had worked in the steel mills for years but had always been forced to commute into the area; housing was all white when the mills were flourishing. When layoffs emptied some homes and reduced the demand, minorities were able to move in. But then unemployment problems became more severe, both at the plants and in all the related businesses in the area, which means virtually every employer. The newcomers were left with few options or resources to fall back on.

Through UNO, the community has met this situation with a realistic approach that tries to take care of the immediate consequences of the problem and generate some community programs for the future without spreading false hopes and promises. UNO helps people develop a firm sense of hope and dignity and gives them a constructive way to address their problems instead of just feeling like victims.

"Overwhelming as they may seem, we know we've got to work on our basic problems like employment," says Ms. Montes. "It's OK to work on all kinds of day-to-day neighborhood needs, and it's OK to work on the Kevin Fest [an annual fair at St. Kevin's Church], but community organizing has to be more than just a fest."

The first objective was to see that unemployment and welfare benefits were provided, and social services made available, in a community that had never before needed such programs. Major public agencies were pushed into setting up appropriate offices and information sources. Through UNO efforts, the community was designated a health manpower shortage area and the city established a new public health clinic. Food pantries were established. UNO gave space, seed money, and organizational support for a new legal clinic providing inexpensive services to clients experiencing the host of personal problems that follow an abrupt loss of income. And a campaign that focused on the fare structure of the Illinois Central Railroad brought a reduction in ticket prices to downtown Chicago, where many of the new job opportunities in the city were.

Of major interest has been skill retraining, given that most of the laid-off workers will never again get the jobs they once had in the mills. Some retraining activity began under the federal Comprehensive Employment and Training Act program. When that funding was eliminated, UNO looked elsewhere for a new resource. City Colleges of Chicago seemed a likely candidate. The record of the city college system had been unimpressive, especially in training programs leading directly to jobs, and there were political pressures for new initiatives. Contrasts were being drawn between city college programs and those of newer suburban community colleges that were closely related to local industry and increasingly effective in producing jobs for suburban workers.

After a persistent UNO campaign, City Colleges of Chicago agreed to build a new type of neighborhood skills center in the area—not a major institution but a local service base offering a flexible program tailor-made to the needs of the community. College administration agreed to move ahead right away rather than wait for construction. Twelve hundred people enrolled immediately in the new courses in temporary facilities. When the new facility opens in early 1988, it will provide a mix of initial retraining opportunities leading to more extensive programs at a nearby campus and other centers in the city. Like its suburban counterparts, City Colleges of Chicago now seeks industry contracts so that as many trainees as possible can expect realistic programs with jobs available upon successful completion.

Efforts by UNO and others to prevent or modify the mill shutdowns themselves have been unsuccessful. The Wisconsin Steel plant has closed and been razed after extensive community attempts to have alternatives considered. The major part of the USX South Works is closed and awaits demolition; sixty-five hundred workers were employed there five years ago. LTV (Republic Steel) recently carried out a major cutback in its work force. Many families have left the community to seek employment elsewhere, but for many others this is home and for both family and financial reasons they stay. Members of such families make up the core of UNO active membership, and they are working on their own community economic development plans for the future. Those plans build pragmatically on what's available, step by step. The new city college skills center is already showing it will be a valuable anchor institution for its particular neighborhood. A fast-food franchise is being built alongside of it, the local commuting train station is being modernized, the Chicago Park District is building a new soccer field thanks to a UNO initiative, and a UNO member church congregation is working on its own plans for building new housing.

When people see these developments coming along step by step, they begin to see possibilities. The different people who have worked hard in these various campaigns are determined to establish some momentum, win some other active participants, and move on together to other opportunities, especially those that will gain new jobs for community people.

Meanwhile UNO had asked a research agency, the Woodstock Institute, to study banking practices in the area, realizing that success in economic development would depend on access to cooperative credit conditions. Woodstock's report described poor banking services in a "credit-starved" community. In a city long without branch banking and therefore dependent on community banks, the report was especially critical of one local financial institution. That bank subsequently worked out an agreement with Federal Reserve Board officials to expand its services and is currently working with UNO on business and housing development plans. At present, it is also contributing $15,000 to a UNO plan to create a housing agency in the community, a project to which the city has also made a modest grant.

"My husband and I often think about moving," Ms. Montes reports. "But I feel a real bond to the community and to UNO. There have been a lot of good personal changes for me, through UNO. I've met so many people, I've experienced so many new things that have added to my life. I've learned how to assert myself, which is something I can use everywhere in daily life. I feel strongly about being part of what's happening in our community, and I want to be here when the real changes come."

One difficulty common to many communities in trouble is their use as dumping grounds. The southeast side of Chicago has already had more than its share of disposal facilities and illegal dumping. Much of it has been toxic; an Illinois EPA report has disclosed high local rates of lung, prostate, and bladder cancer, and critical levels of carcinogens in the area's air and ground water. Faced with plans for a new 289-acre landfill directly adjoining residential neighborhoods, UNO waged a four-year campaign in which it won a citywide moratorium on any expansion of toxic waste dumping, got the city to appoint a task force on the issue, and played a leadership role in bringing this general metropolitan problem to public attention. The task force has developed alternative plans for disposal and has recommended against any more sites close to residential areas. The late Mayor Harold Washington, speaking at a UNO meeting, endorsed the report and said he was specifically opposed to the new landfill in South East Chicago.

"I enjoy the way we can deal with the power brokers," Ms. Montes says. "I never as an individual thought about approaching any of them. But when you have a lot of community people alongside of you, you can see a real possibility of getting what you want.

"For instance, in my neighborhood our alderman is Eddie Vrdolyak [then chairman of the Cook County Democratic Committee]. He was on record approving the permit for the big dump in our community. When we first began organizing against it, the precinct captains were out talking against us, calling us 'commies' and everything else. As more and more of us learned about the issue and worked on it, they began saying maybe the site wasn't so good after all. Then when Mayor Washington introduced an ordinance to prevent the dump, Vrdolyak introduced one too, the very next day!"

The U.S. Army Corps of Engineers recently announced that the firm that had planned the development of the landfill has withdrawn its application. Lots of people are now on the bandwagon, but in the beginning nothing happened until UNO took on the issue and pursued it consistently.

Meanwhile, the faltering economy in the area has jeopardized a community infrastructure that, though stable for generations, has never had resources to spare. UNO and its member groups have focused effective community attention on specific neighborhood needs, some new, some old: preventing cuts in public transportation, gaining school improvements instead of accepting decay, convincing the park district to make repairs and work with residents on new programs, getting new police patrols in trouble spots, proposing a referendum to close down bars in one problem precinct, getting street and sanitation repairs, stopping insurance redlining, and, in the old days of such programs, negotiating with the U.S. Department of Housing and Urban Development for the rehabilitation and sale of abandoned housing.

Activity about the public schools in the area has been especially strong. The old PTAs in the community had been accustomed to a trivial role—"putting on cookie and candy drives to raise money for the school system," as a longtime resident recalls. With a new population that has fewer political ties to ensure relatively good schools, UNO leadership realized that the schools could no longer be expected to perform well without deliberate community participation. Two years ago, UNO recruited twenty-four key parent leaders to attend a series of intensive training sessions, concentrating on both organizational skills and the substance of what is needed to create effective schools. PTA meetings are now more relevant to concerns about education, and more parents come. As an indication of the school system's respect, the president of the Board of Education, two other board members, the deputy superintendent, the field superintendent, and the district superintendent all attended UNO's 1986 convention.

UNO shows persistence and follow-up. After the new health clinic ran into problems because promised services weren't offered, some survey results and recommendations were presented at a UNO meeting with the city health commissioner, and a plan was worked out for improvements. When it became clear that some of the people who most needed the legal clinic weren't using it, UNO and the clinic began holding neighborhood meetings about typical legal problems. A voter registration drive revealed the number of Hispanics who were unregistered because they weren't citizens. Anticipating the present urgent need for such information following the 1986 immigration act, UNO launched a program to help people learn how the naturalization process works, how to apply, and how to get help in making citizenship an achievable dream. And since early experience with the new city college skill training programs has shown how many applicants cannot take advantage of the training because of illiteracy, plans are being developed for reading classes in the neighborhoods.

There is now a larger UNO—the United Neighborhood Organizations of Chicago—in which UNO of South East Chicago and three other predominantly Hispanic organizations are affiliated. This gives each group valuable ties to other sources of community experience and creative ideas; provides centralized training, bookkeeping, and other administrative services; and makes possible more effective work on problems that need to be addressed at least partially on a citywide basis.

UNO of Chicago has built new programs of larger scope on top of two South East Chicago UNO experiences. First, to develop plans for a more ambitious city college skills center on the near southwest side of the city, it organized a distinguished committee of leaders from the four UNO communities; corporate CEOs from Amoco, Illinois Bell, Jewel Companies, and Seaway National Bank; a U.S. senator; the Illinois Senate president and the Speaker of the House; the chancellor of City Colleges of Chicago; and officials from other city agencies.

In its proposal for the project, UNO of Chicago noted that "recently, a civic-minded executive traveled throughout the country attempting to attract investment to Chicago. The number one reason that potential investors gave for not considering Chicago as a business site was the fear of social unrest," due largely to unemployment.

"The only logical response to this deep-rooted problem," the UNO report continued, "is to create community-based education and retraining programs to put some hope into what is presently perceived as a hopeless situation." UNO said that it looked to City Colleges of Chicago to establish a "collaborative effort between government bodies, businesses, the educational institutions, and community groups." Many, many meetings and negotiations later, at a climactic session in one of the UNO neighborhoods, both Mayor Washington and Gov. James Thompson spoke to two thousand community residents and pledged support for the center. Representing an investment of over $50 million, it will be a major new Chicago resource for training a competent work force.

As UNO of Chicago's initial proposal pointed out, referring to both the planned new major skills center and the neighborhood center on the southeast side, "These city college efforts are not conceived to be just new buildings and new programs. Community colleges throughout the country are envisioning themselves as an integral part of an economic strategy for their communities." UNO's campaign has been instrumental in making that point clear in Chicago.

And second, UNO of Chicago has just begun a major initiative concerning Chicago's public schools, gathering together leaders from UNO of South East Chicago and the other affiliates into an education committee that intends to become a well-informed, major participant in what the city has to do in addressing the problems of its school system. Consistent with the way UNO of Chicago and its affiliates see themselves, the proposal for this initiative includes provisions for strengthening the work in local schools as well as for building the larger effort, because the larger effort always depends on the experience and insights gained in neighborhood activity.

The 1987 budget for UNO of South East Chicago is $84,000. Churches are contributing $10,000; benefits and other grass-roots fund-raising yield $10,000; and the balance comes from Chicago-area foundations and corporate giving programs. Nine such sources supported the organization in 1986.

Bruce Orenstein is the executive director of UNO of South East Chicago. The fact that he is the only full-time staff person underscores UNO's determination to have the members themselves do the work of establishing priorities, planning, and carrying out the action programs of the organization. He provides an experienced, professional level of counsel to the member groups about strengthening their own neighborhood activities and coming together around their communitywide agenda. He helps them connect both to effective training and other resources for what they need and to the other UNOs and related organizations they can work with.

Leaders are the life-giving quality of the organization. Thirty-six South East Chicago volunteer leaders went to UNO of Chicago training weekends in 1986 to enhance their effectiveness both for UNO and for the member organizations to which they belong. Five South East Chicago leaders attended weeklong residential training sessions conducted by the Gamaliel Foundation, a new community organizing institute in Chicago to which UNO belongs. More local training sessions were also designed and implemented for UNO of South East Chicago member churches, agencies, schools, and other institutions.

Leadership becomes defined as the constant generation of new leadership. Mary Ellen Montes notes, "There are always people I'm trying to bring along. I urge them to speak up about different issues where they feel strongly and follow through. I promise to support them any way I can. I'm working with five or six right now. I'd like them to feel the same fantastic way I do when we win a victory for the community. It's the high you don't have to take drugs for. . . .

"Everything ties together. If we can keep out another toxic landfill, we can use the new skills center as the centerpiece for a campaign to attract new industry. But it's so frustrating sometimes, so uncertain. When will we know we are safe—no more dumps and they'll clean up what we've got?"

When Ms. Montes said this, she had just read a news story in the morning *Chicago Tribune* that caught her eye with the headline "Firm Seeks to Ship PCBs to South Side." It seems that the same company that had planned the 289-acre landfill had its eye on her UNO neighborhood again. According to the article, the firm was now trying to make arrangements to move "some 2.8 million gallons of cancer-causing PCB wastes" to Chicago from out of town and incinerate them in her community.

Matching the Three Community Organizations Against the Specifications for Participation

How well do these organizations meet the specifications outlined in chapter 4, the characteristics necessary for programs to enhance participation? It's useful to reverse the order of the three specification categories and start with the specific strengths required, move

on to the functions involved, and finish with the eventual results
we are looking for.

Strengths

UNO and MOP get over five hundred people to their annual meetings and involve others in specific activities. BUILD and the four
combined UNOs attract almost three thousand people to meetings.
These may not work out to be high percentages of the whole communities' populations, but they indicate a *significant number of
people* who, at a given moment in their lives, want to be involved.
The disciplined process of organizing within different areas and
among different institutions of the community produces broadly
diversified representation. Those who come to annual meetings
and those who end up serving on committees are accountable to
the constituencies of their own neighborhood institutions. When
MOP leaders in Adams County get "super-empowered," the disciplines of good organizing enforce accountability and broad-based
decision making. Every organizing effort emphasizes openness,
inclusiveness, a sense of belonging, and ownership. Nothing else
presents so many people in the community with such an opportunity for participation in public life.

The approach these organizations use is *holistic*; they deal with
life as it comes in their communities. Practically speaking, members have to single out specific needs and issues to work on, but
they appreciate firsthand how, as Mary Ellen Montes says, "Everything ties together." They can be expected to make more dependable decisions that don't always cause more problems than they
solve because they have the best chance to predict what's going
to happen to whom as a result of those decisions. The interrelat-
edness of different concerns becomes clear: jobs and schools at
BUILD; military spending (and military pollution) and money for
neighborhoods at MOP; toxic wastes, economic development, and
jobs at UNO.

If one believes that the only realistic way to approach human
troubles in community life is from a point of view that sees "the
interconnectedness of different problems and interests," as the

specifications say, then the only people who can be counted on to have that view are the community people themselves, working in their own organizations. It's the key to the creativity community organizations show when they invent new approaches to problems. At BUILD, it was no great trick for the members to see the good sense of getting at school problems by concentrating on the skills and habits employers demand of young people looking for jobs. They know why their young people can't get work.

MOP is a good example of groups designed and determined to be *independent and autonomous*. The churches are parts of denominations, but as far as community affairs are concerned, those parishes and congregations are as independent as the other neighborhood groups that belong to MOP. Their institutional base gives them the organizational wherewithal to keep them from being dependent on anybody. As a set of institutional members, they in turn have authority over their metropolitan network; they all pay dues, elect MOP's board from their own ranks, and set the agenda. Similarly, UNO is independent from the strong political organization whose chairman has been in its midst. UNO is glad to work with anyone who shares its interests on a particular issue, but it avoids entanglements in partisan politics. Independence, incidentally, doesn't mean much if you're strictly second-class citizens anyway; the Commonwealth Agreements confirm BUILD's strength in independence as an equal, essential participant "at the table," as Gary Rodwell says.

Leaders of all three organizations use their own expressive language when talking about the necessity of keeping the *small units* of neighborhood organizing on top, no matter how engrossed some leaders may get in bigger arrangements. "My new friends are silver plated, my old friends are gold," says Dolores Martinez of MOP. Ms. Montes talks first about building small neighborhood groups; she then describes how UNO "enlarges the circle" but emphasizes that the local autonomy remains. Mr. Rodwell describes the "double-edged sword" BUILD has to have: "The larger organization is only as strong as the individual churches." And BUILD's Commonwealth Agreement strategy ends up back in small units

in the neighborhoods, where people will work as volunteers on
the high school community committees. The leaders of these organizations know from their own experience how right economist
Mancur Olson was: when you get too big and fancy, you get remote and lose people.

From a staff point of view, Mike Kromrey shows the attitude
essential to his work with the individual neighborhood components
of a community organization: "These are respectable existing institutions. We have to earn the right to work with them."

All three organizations invest substantially in *skills training for
both leadership and staff*—skills in organizing and communicat-
ing, skills in identifying problems and inventing solutions. The experienced staff directors they have hired, the outside help they contract for, and the positions they give to leaders with experience
and insight reflect the importance they place on skills necessary
to a community organization.

All three organizations have a lot of poor people in their constituencies. All three raise money in their communities but win *enabling support from outside resources*. All three have minimal budgets; more support could provide more depth in organizing in the
neighborhoods.

Functions

The three examples typify how community organizations are always bringing people together to (1) *discuss their circumstances
and form ideas*, (2) *focus attention and take responsibility*, and (3)
move on to action and learn from the experience. The organizing
processes at BUILD, MOP, and UNO are all aimed at stimulating
that kind of participation. Meetings are endemic, epidemic. There's
an old expression: it sometimes seems that community organizations will never work because there aren't enough evenings in the
week, or enough coffee and doughnuts, or enough flyers about meetings to tuck between everyone's doorknob and doorjamb.

It's not all meetings. Sometimes it's research, with as many people
involved as possible. As a leader in MOP, Vicki Ceja didn't go
out by herself and become an expert on zoning and then come back

and tell the people in the community what to do. As she says, "We all went out and learned about what was going on and what we could do about it." Similarly, Ms. Montes of UNO doesn't deal with politicians all by herself. The way she refers to the experience shows her involvement in good organizing: "As more and more of us learned about the issue and worked on it...." Then there are other times when responsibility has to be given to specific individuals in the group. As Mr. Rodwell says, "You depend on good people from the community to see that their own views and those of others are heard."

Learning by experience and feeding new insights back into the community is ultimately the mark of a vigorous community organization sincerely interested in community progress. The deliberate procedure UNO follows in developing its agenda not only gives everyone a chance to feel a part of decision making; it also provides time for learning about the issues involved and what can be done. The way UNO has persisted in follow-up, insisting that those in charge of new programs tinker with their inner workings till they get them right, is another example of how good community organizations keep nibbling away at problems. So is Mr. Rodwell's insistence that BUILD's long-term responsibilities in making the Commonwealth Agreements work are just beginning. BUILD keeps reviewing, revising, and pushing ahead again. These organizations know there are no quick and easy 100 percent solutions to the real problems in their communities. You have to take a step, learn, and take another.

There are five MOP issues mentioned in the description here, and all five represent concerns—and victories—that are *both private and public*. The mud slides, the threat of displacement, the contaminated water supply, the need for more responsive utility practices, and the need for better schools for everybody's children were all matters affecting citizens privately but which had to be addressed in broader public community terms to be resolved. The fact that private needs get met through public life is the major answer to the economists' dilemmas noted in chapter 2; in this community activity, private and public motivations are not separate but interwoven. As Mr. Rodwell says, "to galvanize all of us, you have to respect our self-interests." Community organizations help people develop what Robert Dahl values as the "enlightened understanding of [one's] best self-interest." In the unique community context of these organizations, self-interests tend to be expressed at the less mean, more public-spirited end of the scale. Thomas Jefferson's nephew, Peter Carr, would have enjoyed belonging to these groups.

Victories bring confidence and vision. Ms. Ceja's involvement at MOP began with the mud in her street, moved on to the housing troubles of another nearby neighborhood, and then spread to metropolitan campaigns such as the work on utility rates and the quality of the region's schools. But it was the beginning, getting rid of the mud, that "got us to thinking about what we could accomplish."

Victories also bring joy and solidarity: "It's the high you don't have to take drugs for." Others in the community see leaders such as Ms. Montes gaining satisfaction from being involved and winning respect and friends, and they want some of the same. That nudge provides what Olson calls "selective incentives," the personal motivations he recognizes as realistic reasons to participate.

The three organizations introduce their members to all sorts of new *connections with people outside* their local communities. MOP's "spice of life" relationships between Adams County and Denver people are the first such ties in the area; as Ms. Ceja says, "It opens us up." MOP leaders' "super-empowerment" and Ms. Montes's heady experience with the political system are typical of the way community organizing brings people face to face with major institutions and political actors, with enough community support to build confidence. It's always a surprise. As Reverend Miles of BUILD says, "I never envisioned being able to get the ear of the city's corporate and political elite. BUILD has changed all that."

Results

Ms. Montes's comments speak to the six specifications for results. UNO has given her an *enthusiasm for public life* that keeps her in the community. She finds *competence and strength* she never knew she had, and that makes for growth. She works first with all sorts of people in her own neighborhood and then in the larger circles of UNO. The whole experience builds *understanding and respect*: "Organizing to solve problems makes us closer; it's a good feeling. . . . "We're better off together than we are alone."

Encouraging her neighbors to get involved and become leaders is a natural everyday activity. Judging by her experience with Chairman Vrdolyak, she's certainly learning how to build *robust relationships with elected representatives*. She's serious about UNO *concentrating on the urgent problems of the increasingly poor neighborhoods* of South East Chicago.

The others in our examples confirm the way community organizing produces these impacts. Ms. Ceja reflects on enthusiasm and competence in public life when she speaks of how "people in that neighborhood now know they have something to work for. . . . I've learned how the system works . . . . The most important thing is for people to be able to look at a problem and say, 'Hey, we can do something about that!' "

Mr. Rodwell's experience attests to mutual understanding and respect: "[We can] touch the lives of other people." It is impressive to see the working relationships BUILD and UNO have developed with corporate leadership, respecting the role business has to play in winning change.

Ms. Martinez discusses leadership development: "You can't let people put you in the position of taking credit by just accepting their thanks . . . . You've got to respond with the truth—that it wouldn't have happened without them being involved . . . . We always have to be looking for new leaders, . . . finding the people others respect, offering support and training."

Regarding relationships with elected representatives, Ms. Ceja notes, "We elected them, and we figure we've got the best chance to make them work for us."

And Mr. Rodwell speaks to the necessity of effective participation in poor communities, compared with the alternative of being excluded: "It can't go on that way, with the majority of the population not getting a commensurate share of the progress."

The leaders quoted here and others like them are among the most valuable citizens we have in this country—not just for BUILD, MOP, and UNO but also for the many other activities they become involved in within and beyond their own local communities. They and all the others who are active in these organizations are not "so inert, so averse to activity," to recall C.B. Macpherson's phrase of despair. Their experiences reflect personal invigoration and growth, which we've seen to be a healthy product of proper participation in public life. There is a solid consistency in how they approach their roles. They have worked their way up into sophisticated endeavors about major issues, but they always have one foot firmly planted back home where they keep persuading others to become active. That's the key to their value as leaders, and it comes from a clear understanding of the disciplines of good community organizing.

Mr. Rodwell's comments about Baltimore are reminiscent of the earlier description of communities under pluralism. There is a certain equilibrium within at least the half of the city that is experiencing a renaissance. It is moving along on a course that appears to be progress. A lot looks good and prosperous. Of course, those directly involved in implementing the progress encounter occasional disagreements, but they compromise and settle such troubles without upsetting the basic equilibrium. It's important that any major issues outside the pragmatic day-by-day scope of renaissance be avoided, and this includes the circumstances and concerns of the other half of the "two cities" that are Baltimore. Few people raise any serious objections to what's happening. Most don't participate in public life, especially not in any way that encourages them to reflect on matters of values or formulate a realistic view of the future for the city and all the people who live in it.

BUILD intervenes and upsets the equilibrium because in its members' firsthand view of the city, Baltimore clearly "can't go on that way." They are convinced that the avoidance of basic troubles is eventually going to fail. Thus, they take a position of civic leadership and ask others to join them in addressing those troubles.

Troubles include the fact that neither the schools nor their students are performing satisfactorily. As the *News-American* editorial suggests, the condition of the schools is obviously not a new problem. It is, as Robert Dahl described such situations, one of those "major public problems [that] go unsolved because every solution that does not have substantial agreement among all the organizational forces is, in effect, vetoed." BUILD's role is to take the initiative against that familiar stalemate of pluralism and offer a better bargain to those organizational forces—government, business, labor, institutions—so they will begin to pay attention and take constructive action.

It can be said that BUILD, MOP, and UNO are interest groups in the terminology of chapter 2, but they are interest groups with some differences. They are eager to include values in the conversation. Mr. Rodwell speaks of "the values we have around our families, our religious life and the workplace." Their interests are not narrowly defined to fit into one of pluralism's special interest slots. Their context is the community as a whole, their members can make the connections between different facets of community life, and their leaders don't have just a thin slice of their constituents' attention but deliberately stay close to the whole of community life right along with everyone else.

The business report cited by UNO identified a major consideration that inhibits industrial development in Chicago: "fear of social unrest." Similar reports could be written about many other parts of the country. In a pluralist mindset, there doesn't seem to be any answer to that problem or even the chance to talk about it constructively. Except for occasional dire predictions, it is unmentionable; out of scope. Only when the conversation is made broader and more lively, when there is talk about "the values of what's important to people" as Mr. Rodwell says, can there be the beginnings of solutions. BUILD, MOP, and UNO start those conversations for us.

If one looks for ideology in their work, it's not one of Republicans and Democrats but a more fundamental conviction about self-responsibility and self-determination—the prime importance of people taking charge of their lives and communities.

Compared with more modest community organizations elsewhere, BUILD, MOP, and UNO may seem so big and well established that they are poor models. It needs to be emphasized just once more that the strength and unique character of all three is in their small-scale roots among neighborhood people and neighborhood institutions. If the base isn't there, with authority, there can be no legitimate larger enterprise. In all places—including Baltimore, Denver, and Chicago—there is ample work to do in encouraging the establishment of that neighborhood base.

I spoke earlier of the indispensable role of participation "to keep new life flowing in the democratic system" and called that participation a working patriotism, which would contribute mightily to the security of this country and the protection of its citizens. The three organizations described here and others like them will—with some help—generate that participation.

PART TWO:

THE RESPONSE
OF PHILANTHROPY

CHAPTER 6

ROOTS OF OUR HABITS

So if community organizations are so great, why haven't funding sources been tripping over each other offering money in the field? Why isn't there a community organization in every poor neighborhood in the country, supported by philanthropists who are daily becoming more sensitive and sophisticated about how such organizations benefit both the people in those communities and all the rest of us as well? Why do impressive organizations like BUILD, MOP, and UNO have to work so hard to raise modest budgets?

To answer this, we will look at how some habits in and around philanthropy inhibit the support of community organizations, in the hope of offering some suggestions about modifying those habits. A good place to begin is among the inherited traits of our philanthropic traditions.

In Italy during the fourteenth and fifteenth centuries, a system of private philanthropy was established to take care of the *poveri vergognosi*—literally, the "shamed poor," but also known as the genteel poor, the fallen elite, the "fatter poor," or "men and women which are of good families decayed"—those who were of the higher socioeconomic classes but happened to be down on their luck at the moment and too ashamed to beg.

The truly "miserable," on the other hand, were the indigents of lower classes, and the orphans, widows, and crippled of all classes. It was assumed that they weren't ashamed to beg or accept handouts publicly; they had no alternative. Thus, they could be a more public responsibility, receiving whatever pittance of assistance was available.

Any large gift to charity, any gift of quality food or clothing or housing, was for the *poveri vergognosi*. As a matter of law, the words *poor* and *poverty* were reserved for this class, rather than for the miserables. The poor were thusly defined as those of good position who didn't have "those things required to live rightly. . . . Unless he has enough tờ live well and blessedly, he is called poor." To help such a person in his hour of need was an act that demonstrated one's sense of social responsibility. "If you want honor," said a contemporary, "you have to give to some poor gentlemen."

Private confraternities were set up to handle this brand of charity. They became large, attractive membership agencies in which money, goods, and properties were collected from members and other peers. Some aid was gained through a stylish form of anonymous begging: the poor confraternity member, or a more fortunate member volunteering his time for the benefit of other members, wore a mask or veil to hide his identity. His class, however, was easily recognized from his dress so that his peers could be confident about where their contributions were going.

It isn't hard for us to project ourselves back five hundred years and see how this early form of organized private philanthropy became so appealing. As you met the masked confraternity member, your heart reached out to someone basically like you. Counting your blessings that it wasn't you who was in trouble, you took comfort in thinking you and your family would be taken care of if it became your turn next time. Historian Richard Trexler waxes poetic as he visualizes this act of charity; he says that you the donor could identify with the masked victim and recognize yourself "beneath the veil." And you could feel confident the gift would not be wasted but used wisely, just as it would be if you yourself were the recipient.

Such have always been the inclinations of most philanthropists to make their contributions among their peers, one way or another. Funding peers instead of the poor is one of three peculiarities to be addressed in this chapter. The other two are funding private institutional development and professional authority and funding the medical model. All three are old, well-entrenched philanthropic habits that catch up with us today and tend to limit philanthropic enthusiasm for the type of community organizations represented by BUILD, MOP, and UNO. Our purpose is not to pass judgment on past practice but rather to see how the roots of such habits square with current conditions and philanthropic opportunities.

Funding Peers Instead of the Poor

Participation in America isn't just for the rich or the poor but for everybody. It goes without saying that that's the way it should be. However, now we're talking more specifically about *philanthropic* support for such participation. In that context, people with good jobs and incomes may need community organizations to encourage them to become active participants in American public life. It may take hard work to create those arrangements, but a lack of money is not a problem standing in their way. When they want to get organized, relatively well-to-do citizens have the modest financial resources required to help make things happen.

Communities of poor people, on the other hand, do not. Some essential items, which are simply handled as volunteered contributions in more affluent communities, become significant organizational expenses in poor communities. These may include phone calls, stamps, gas, bus and baby-sitting money, or money for coffee and rolls. Few members have easy access to Xerox machines at the office. Such prosaic items are basic necessities to a community organization. Without them, and without the outside support that makes them available, the work doesn't get done.

Then there is the need for organizing and management skills. Some people are natural leaders in any community. But they still need certain organizing and management skills in order to use their natural abilities successfully in addressing community issues. Many middle-class people get exposed to some of these skills in their on-the-job and extracurricular experiences, but that doesn't happen so much in poor communities. Good training programs, access to experienced groups elsewhere, and competent staff can bring leaders together and help them gain the capacities necessary to work effectively on the problems of their communities.

Support is needed to pay for training for community people, to pay staff, to pay some essential expenses, to pay for whatever is necessary to enable the community to begin making up for what it has been lacking in effective human resources required for moving ahead.

As a role for philanthropy, that may sound as though it makes a lot of sense, but the truth is that it's been hard for community organizations in poor communities to raise money. Of the three examples in chapter 5, MOP has relied heavily on the in-kind support it gets from Denver Catholic Community Services for its organizing staff. That help has been cut, however, and MOP has had little success in winning consistent funding from other sources. There was some local foundation and corporate support in the beginning but, as so often happens, grants ran out and were not renewed. BUILD lost what few major corporate contributions it had in Baltimore and its cynicism about support from foundations and corporations—an attitude partly of "It's not worth trying" and partly of distrust—is common in the field. Hard times raising money was one of the compelling reasons why UNO of South East Chicago decided to cut its staff and depend on UNO of Chicago for more efficient centralized administrative services. And this was in Chicago, where there is more understanding and support among funders about organizing than anywhere else.

So it's important to look at the choices philanthropy has made with respect to poor people and their community needs. In Italy, as we've seen, the philanthropy of the confraternities stayed in the middle class and helped preserve the more prosperous families of the communes. Much the same thing happened in England a century later within the powerful livery companies—the trade associations organized to help their memberships of craftsmen. Going back a bit further, perhaps the general purpose was the same in the ancient world; at least the behavior was the same. In the private giving of corn, oil, and cash in Greece and Rome

> the poorest class of society was never singled out for specially favourable treatment, although where the amount to be distributed was large enough, they might be treated on an equal footing with the more well-to-do, more especially when the occasion was of a religious character. . . . However, where the amount which a person had to give was on a lesser scale (and it was only a few men who could give a really worthwhile gift to everyone. . .), the money was likely to go to the town-councillors or to that particular section of the upper class to which the donor himself belonged. . . . The distribution was thus confined to those held 'worthy of honour.'

Many of our American traditions are similar, if not so explicit. Perhaps it was not so much so in the very beginning. In our earliest rural and small-town life, people of varying means were neighbors and had many occasions to become familiar with one another. The community spirit was often generous and was expressed in private philanthropy. As economist Alan Batchelder says, "Knowing the poor, the nonpoor extended charity. . . . The nonpoor knew of the problems of the poor as the problems of their neighbors." Those early American settlers who did well had great enthusiasm for the potential the new land offered everybody; a small direct gift to help one less fortunate to climb the first step toward economic independence must have seemed a first-rate charitable investment.

But we quickly became a less intimate society. In his thoughtful book about asylums, David J. Rothman proposes that, in the eighteenth and nineteenth centuries, as the poor became less frequently familiar neighbors of the well-off in the new nation, they became instead "a social problem, a potential source of unrest, and the proper object of a reform movement." This movement recommended that the poor be removed from the community and placed in public poorhouses, which we had not had in any significant number during colonial times.

By the middle 1800s, government agencies had taken on much of the responsibility for the needy in poorhouses, orphanages, insane asylums, reformatories, and penitentiaries. Private philanthropy could turn to a different mission. Ironically enough, the new mission was to help the well-to-do realize an improvement in the quality of their lives that had been learned from the poor.

Here, as in Europe, hospitalization was originally only for the poor. *Hôpitals* in France and their counterparts here and elsewhere were workhouses or almshouses for the poor, which at least purported to treat illness and injury when the need arose among their residents. The poor who had avoided institutionalization were also served in these places, if anywhere. Middle- and upper-class people, on the other hand, considered themselves fortunate in being able to be attended to at home. As medical science progressed, however, doctors and their more affluent patients came to believe that in this instance the poor were not so unfortunate after all, at least not in the way they were hospitalized when sick. It seemed as though medical care needed its own facilities outside the home. Thus began the development of voluntary hospitals, so called because support for these hospitals for the more affluent came voluntarily rather than through taxes. Ever since, private hospitals have won a large share of private philanthropic giving. Although they have accepted some charity cases, their economics and their social position have always made them lean toward a higher class of patients whenever such patients have been available. Once more, private philanthropy settled into a role largely benefiting the nonpoor.

A unique characteristic of giving became part of the quality of these contributions and remains so today: most gifts are made in exchange for services to the donor and those with whom he or she identifies. We volunteer our major contributions to private hospitals, the United Way, universities, and all sorts of other services because we want these resources to be there when we or our families, employees, friends, or neighbors need them. We just generally feel it is better to have these familiar services available in the private sector, rather than to rely on public, government-run, tax-funded services, which we assume are tailored more to the needs of poor people.

Our private contributions to private services, like the support of the *poveri vergognosi*, are sensible transactions that remind us of the economic model of chapter 2. We saw that, in pluralism, most participation is limited to those who have economic strengths with which to bargain. Just so, our systems of exchange between private philanthropy and private institutions tend to keep most of the fruits of private philanthropy out of the reach of the poor.

Not entirely, of course. There are church groups, social service agencies, and scholarship funds, for instance, which concentrate on trying to help poor people, and there are loyal contributors who support them. But as a share of the total private philanthropy dollar, such support represents a very small percentage.

Economist William Vickrey has made one of the few studies available about who benefits from philanthropy. He analyzes how contributions to churches, universities, and most other institutions and agencies tend to be gifts that benefit others of the same social strata as the contributor. He concludes that, overall, "the difference in economic level between donor and beneficiary is comparatively small." Kenneth Boulding, the noted economist who has focused considerable attention on questions of public and private social welfare payments, speaks specifically of foundations: "One suspects that foundation grants benefit immediately the middle-income and upper-income classes and only indirectly benefit the poor."

We all recognize the fundamental virtues of the act of giving. A gift to a worthwhile organization "is no less generous" if that organization happens to serve middle-class people. We find satisfaction in making contributions to those established institutions that are governed by people we respect. We enjoy supporting livelihoods for professors, artists, medical researchers, social workers, and other professional people who seem to stand for the qualities in our culture to which all citizens, rich and poor, should aspire. Appeals from such causes are and always have been attractive. Proposals from organizations run by the citizens of poor communities have a hard time competing.

But there can be some surprising modifications in these perspectives during a time such as now, when contributors are more apt to plan, establish objectives, figure costs and benefits, and look for ways in which scarce funds can really make a difference. When one looks at giving from these more deliberate approaches, grants to community organizations of poor people may be no more generous than the support of anything else, but they can soon be seen as more crucial with respect to the lives of the beneficiaries. In giving significant assistance to those who especially need it and have the fewest other resources to turn to, such philanthropy may not be more generous, but it is more charitable and its leverage is greater.

Further, although the poor may no longer be neighbors of philanthropists, the cultural distance in some ways may not be so great as it once was. Abraham Maslow and others have made us more aware of the similarities in values and needs among all people. We know we have in common a bundle of basic wants and fears, and at the moment we are probably better than we used to be at recognizing and expressing them. The arts, entertainment, and advertising have become media of enormous cultural exchange in this country. Poor people have adopted habits and perspectives of others, and in turn they have given the rest of the country contributions in language and the arts, for instance, which make up much of our national vitality. Without minimizing the differences in our comforts and urgencies, it is possible for donors to find peers among the poor to an extent unrealizable in the days when philanthropic habits were born.

All three community organizations described previously are zeroing in on the problems of public schools, largely with respect to minority children from low-income families. Finding ways in which schools can do a better job of helping these children learn and grow is a movement whose time has come, and it will be interesting to see if we all can recognize how interrelated our best self-interests are in this case. The quality of all our children's educations is reduced, and the cost increased, when school for some is a dismal failure. All parents are peers.

Among these peers will be poor people who share with philanthropists many middle-class values about behavior. In Chicago's rich community organization traditions, for instance, there are many examples of how organizing has persuaded steady leadership people to stay in poor communities by involving them as leaders and helping them own their own homes, get insurance, reduce crime, and generally make the community habitable. The finest moment for an organizer is when a leader decides to stay and work, as did Mary Ellen Montes of UNO. Such leaders contribute tremendously to whatever level of stability and working order exists in the community; their role can be recognized, appreciated, and encouraged by those involved in philanthropy.

Finally, for those still looking for the fallen elite to give to, as in fourteenth-century Italy, such candidates are very much with us today. They are those American workers who are unemployed because of shifts in production, imports, antiquated facilities, automation, and other unsettling characteristics of our industrial economy. They are called the "new poor." One of the early objectives of UNO and organizations like it has been to see that such constituents are not a shamed poor but rather are men and women who are determined to take charge of their own destinies and find ways to recover and prosper. Modern-day philanthropic resources can help them in this pursuit through contributions to organizations such as UNO.

Funding Private Institutional Development and Professional Authority

It is interesting to see how different our early American institutions were from the image we assume. Until the early 1800s, Harvard was not at all a private, independent institution as we know and value that form today. It was governed by a variety of church-state arrangements, and 55 percent of its support came from the government. At Yale the figure was 70 percent.

The popularizing and secularizing of government in this country slowly changed those arrangements. In his book *The Organization of American Culture, 1700–1900*, Peter Dobkin Hall traces the way members of the aristocracy lost their old, unquestioned authority in government and the power that went with it, and had to find a new institutional base. They found it by inventing what we now call the private sector. The unique design of the American private corporation was born—first in charity, then in business.

The new private institutions grew rapidly in resources and influence. Private stewardship of distinguished universities, hospitals, social service agencies, and arts organizations became the guardian of established, enlightened tradition outside of government—a tradition that began to have a great impact on our political as well as cultural development. The institutions and the leading citizens who controlled them formed an important part of our checks and balances between public and private realms— something we came to value as a uniquely American characteristic.

In becoming the essential funding ingredient to make the private not-for-profit sector possible, private philanthropy in America had found its principal role. It had also found its most effective appeal. The assurance that funds, once given, would remain in private hands and strengthen the private sector became the strongest underlying appeal in American institutional fund raising.

Much of the new private support for institutions went for bricks and mortar. Thomas Jefferson is among those who have questioned the dominant institutional role for private giving. Always prejudiced against the cities and their urbane institutions, which took young people away from the country and small towns, he recalled later his dismay with the invention of institutional philanthropy: "Even the charities of the nation forgot that misery was their object, and spent themselves in founding schools to transfer to science the hardy sons of the plow."

Such sentiments had little effect. The waves of university, college, and school development; the surge of enthusiasm for voluntary hospitals; the understandable urge to build the new nation's museums and concert halls; the need for church construction; and the pressure to create a system of private social service agencies—all these desires for institutional growth have monopolized American private philanthropy in the nineteenth and twentieth centuries. The late 1800s were especially noteworthy. There was a "vast surplus of wealth," to use Eduard Lindeman's phrase, in the hands of those who had most fully realized the American potential for profit from property and industry—a surplus that "was not needed for purposes of reinvestment." Gifts from the fortunes of Rockefeller, Carnegie, Duke, and their contemporaries set a high standard for massive institutional development. Foundations, churches, corporations, and individual philanthropists have since been following their lead. Private stewardship has remained strong and attractive.

Once established, the institutions have had insatiable appetites for operating funds. We tend to anthropomorphize our institutions; they become needy just like people, and we feel a charitable impulse to respond. Getting back to our medieval Italians, Richard Trexler quotes a lawyer, F. Petrucci, who could just as well be raising money today instead of in the fourteenth century. He justified the decision that his cause, a nunnery, "can be numbered among the poor" by reasoning:

> If it is said that the nunnery has many possessions, we respond that it also has many expenses. Once one considers the nunnery's social and religious position, it can be said that the nunnery is more indigent than the poor mendicant, who is accustomed to begging for his bread in the market place. Only after considering the quality of the poor should alms be distributed accordingly.

In the United States, college presidents, clergymen, hospital administrators, social workers, museum directors, development consultants, and all sorts of dedicated, well-positioned volunteers have pursued lines of reasoning much like Petrucci's and won legend-

ary successes in raising money. They and their benefactors have
given this country a resource of private institutions unique in the
world. The fact that this resource is an ever-mounting financial
burden leads to the irony of government funding. To some extent
we end up back where Harvard began, having to give a different
answer to the question of whether our private institutions ought
to be supported with public as well as private money. For most
private institutions, survival seems to depend in varying degrees
on public support, directly or indirectly. This dependency makes
the philanthropic proposition less appealing because it is less purely
and heroically private and because it is risky to give to an institution dependent on funding that is hardly dependable.

A Twentieth Century Fund report on the performing arts shows
how times have changed and how institutional development has
become risky business for philanthropy instead of the safe investment it used to be or at least appeared to be. Martin Mayer, writing for the fund's Task Force on Performing Arts Centers, speaks
with alarm about two seemingly contradictory things happening
at once: a "mounting financial crisis in the performing arts" and
an "explosion" in the numbers of cultural centers for housing these
activities—centers which in many cases are not going to be economically viable. He sees a "rapid deterioration in the financial
condition of the performing arts" and—writing in 1970—looks to
"expanding federal aid" for a significant part of the solution. In
the 1980s, although government support for the arts has not been
cut the way it has been for social services, enough of an increase
to meet the needs Mayer describes seems unlikely. A lot of noble
institutions, and the philanthropic investments that have made them
possible, seem very much at risk.

Philanthropists have also watched contributions turn questionable in the hospital field. Empty beds have come to signify both
overconstruction and, more recently, radical changes in the length
of hospital stays imposed by prohibitive costs. Unnecessary dupli-
cation of expensive special services, often made possible by ambitious fund-raising drives, has been a factor in pushing hospital
costs out of the reach of all the support systems designed to make
these institutions economically feasible. For-profit hospitals, like
other proprietary service organizations, increasingly compete for
customers without benefit of charitable giving, and that success

leads us to wonder what the role of private philanthropy really is in these fields. Figures on iatrogenic illnesses and injuries—those coming from exposure to health risks *inside* hospitals—make us less sure about hospitals being the best place to get well, anyway. Observations and insights such as these are distressing to generous people who assumed that contributing to the development of institutions such as hospitals was the conservative, unquestioned, blue-chip way to invest philanthropic dollars.

The professionalization of services made possible by philanthropy has run alongside the development of institutions, but the two haven't always been hand in hand. Strength has been steadily increasing among doctors, teachers, social workers, some groups of artists, and other professionals as they have become organized occupational categories, and that strength has brought tremendous change in the way institutions have to operate and be financed.

The institutions themselves have helped make it happen. Board members and others in charge have usually pushed for a more formal and deliberate style, and the professional workers to whom they have turned to carry out this process have taken the theme of formality and played it back in ways not always anticipated. They have won strong professional control of their work. They are not willing to take their rewards in just the virtues of providing service and inspiration to the rest of us. They wish to be respected and paid accordingly. Foundations and other contributors have encouraged this tendency, often unwittingly, by emphasizing the merits of more businesslike practices, which lead to more businesslike payrolls.

Barry Karl cites the example of how the Ford Foundation made grants totaling $80,200,000 in 1966 "to consolidate the nation's rich orchestra resources," as the foundation's annual report said that year. Sixty-one symphony orchestras received a combination of outright support plus endowment grants that had to be matched with funds raised from other sources. Primary aims of the program included "to enable more musicians to devote their major energies to performance" and "to attract more young talent to orchestra careers by raising the income and prestige of the players."

The Ford grants and all the matching grants were indeed effective; they helped create a new conception of what it means to be a performing member of a symphony orchestra. No longer would

musicians be forced to depend heavily on other jobs for their livelihoods. Performing in a good orchestra became a reasonably well-
paid, respectable, professional occupation in itself.

The grants were not made in a vacuum. Symphony managers
were showing Ford the mounting pressures from musicians for
longer seasons, higher salaries, better fringe benefits—the costs
of professionalization, which the orchestras couldn't afford without
massive help. The Ford program became very influential in determining how those pressures would be met and how the relationships between management and musicians would be played out in
the future. Higher levels of costs were established.

Milton R. Bass, looking at the experience from the vantage point
of Tanglewood, where the Boston Symphony Orchestra performs
in the summer, wrote in 1969:

> The Ford Foundation grants of a few years ago, which sup-
> posedly were going to put them on a secure basis, have
> only succeeded in putting the symphonies in a more precar-
> ious position. The musicians, who had been grossly un-
> derpaid for years, demanded and got substantial raises. This
> ate up most of the grants. Meanwhile, other costs were
> skyrocketing while Symphony Hall remained the same size
> and, consequently, could not take in much more income
> through tickets.... People started talking about the end
> of an era.

In all cities where they have been able to assume the new levels
of spending, symphony orchestras have mounted remarkable fund-
raising efforts to do so. These orchestras today most likely are taking
a considerably larger share of private giving than they used to take.
This is not necessarily a bad thing; it's just a good illustration of
how the demands of both professional and institutional development have applied pressures on philanthropy, and of how the funding
sources themselves become part of the process in ways that we don't
talk about in annual reports. It's a good illustration because the
Ford Foundation amounts were so big, at least for their time. Grants
are made every day by smaller foundations that nudge in the same
direction.

Douglas Yates is a veteran professional and administrator who
is clear about how the professionals are in charge in his field, the

social services. He writes that basically we have made a decision in this country that "service delivery should not be based on *an exchange of mutual adjustment with citizens* but on *the authority and expertise of those who deliver services* [author's emphasis]." Philanthropy is attracted to that professional leadership. When it does choose to try to help poor people, it prefers to fund professionals in their service occupations rather than to fund any initiatives that come largely from poor people themselves.

Community organizations typified by the three examples in chapter 5 are not part of this mainstream of institutional development and professional authority. They present few if any opportunities for grants to bricks and mortar; members of their boards of directors are not socioeconomic peers of people who give away money; and the role of the professional staff person is different. In community organization work, community leaders—laypeople—rather than staff have to be in charge or the whole effort is meaningless. It is to *their* authority that a philanthropist contributes.

Because of that unique characteristic, community organizations give contributors a rare opportunity to give in the old-fashioned American way—more directly to people in communities—so as to have that "exchange of mutual adjustment with citizens." It needn't take all of American philanthropy (what a fantasy!), but it can begin to correct the imbalances.

Funding the Medical Model

The chance to give to peers in trouble had one other attraction for the fourteenth-century Italians, one that is probably more recognizable among those of us active in philanthropy than it would be to historian Trexler. Those Italian charities for the shamed poor were an early form of what Barry Karl calls the popular "medical model" of philanthropy. One wasn't throwing money into the bottomless pit of aid for the miserables of society. That was a neverending, thankless task that had to be done to prevent social disturbances as well as to reduce suffering, but it could be handled as a public communal responsibility. One's own private giving was more suited to fixing something that could be fixed, solving a solvable problem, finding a cure, or confronting a particular tragedy that could be overcome, preferably in a program that had some social importance and would pay off in a reasonably short length of time. Attending to those who already had social advantages but were in financial trouble and helping them get back on their feet had this quality. It was an investment that had a much better chance to yield tangible and immediate benefits, benefits that could then be celebrated by donors and donees alike because their loyalties to one another were being well served.

The medical model has continued to be a strong force in philanthropy. In medicine itself, grants for work against polio, typhoid, yellow fever, malaria, and tuberculosis are consistently among the first achievements to be mentioned in any account of American philanthropy. The 1910 Flexner Report on medical education was initiated by the American Medical Association through the Carnegie Foundation for the Advancement of Teaching. It recommended that the prime work of medical schools change from just the study of medical practice to problem solving—research about cures and prevention. The report was widely accepted and became a guide for the philanthropic community as well as a mandate to the medical schools.

In the same year, Andrew Carnegie established the Carnegie Endowment for International Peace to "hasten the abolition of international war, the foulest blot upon our civilization." Carnegie had so much faith in the medical model of philanthropy that he was concerned about what the endowment might do with itself once "war is discarded as disgraceful to civilized men." The endowment is still active and useful, though shy of its goal.

Perhaps the quintessential expression of the medical model is Edwin Embree's book, *Investment in People*, which tells the story of the highly regarded Julius Rosenwald Fund, active from 1917 to 1948 when, by choice, it had given away all its principal. Embree, who became president of the foundation in 1928 when Mr. Rosenwald reorganized the board, used a wonderful expression when he wrote that, from the beginning, the new directors didn't want to leave behind just "a pleasant philanthropic dew." Rather, they wished the foundation to "mobilize all its resources—financial, intellectual, moral—for systematic attack on specific problems." At the end of the book, Embree sums it up:

> Foundations have a special opportunity. . . . They can as-
> semble the keenest minds from all over the world and pro-
> vide stimulating settings for their work. As procedures are
> demonstrated and established, they will be supported by
> the state and community, [so that] foundations, turning to
> new fields, can continue to serve at the frontiers of progress.

It has always been the dream: philanthropy can slay each of society's dragons as it appears and then move on to the next. Those
fine hopes have been repeatedly dashed, yet faith gets reborn time
after time in each day's proposals and grants. Probably today's most
impressive testimony to the appeal of projects that promise to fix
something is the format recommended by the Grantsmanship Center
for applications to foundations and other resources. For almost
twenty years the center has been the leading agency in helping not-
for-profit organizations get organized and raise money. What it suggests as a principal thrust for this recommended format is not a
description of the organization and what it stands for but rather
a "problem statement or needs assessment" that "documents the
needs to be met or problems to be solved by the proposed funding."

The center suggests that this needs assessment immediately zero
in on the specific concern of the proposal so that it "focuses on
the conditions in the lives of your clients or constituents that you
wish to change." It urges the applying organization to choose its
problem carefully: "It should be of reasonable dimensions—a concern that you can realistically do something about over the course
of the grant."

Then the proposal, according to the center's recommendations,
should state the applicant's objectives in addressing the problem—
specifically not "long-range benefits" expressed in "imprecise and
flowery terms" but well-defined "outcomes" that, on the basis of
past experience, can be achieved within a given length of time with
the help of the grant being solicited. Next should come an "explicit" description of the methods to be used in doing just that.

The proposal in this form offers a contract that almost sounds
like it carries a guarantee. If the foundation will provide the funds
required, the applicant agrees to solve a social, health, education,
or whatever problem by isolating it and addressing it in the predetermined fashion described. Regardless of what life in the real world

may hold in store for the grantee and its clientele, the contract is safe and sound for the foundation. What it has bought or invested in is the proposal. To a considerable degree, what happens here is the philanthropic equivalent of the pluralist process. Issues have been cut down and narrowed to a point where they are workable, where one can talk about them confidently in the context of the proposal, regardless of whether the proposal or the conversation has much currency in actual community life, and where some payoff can be looked for in, say, the customary three years of grant support.

These comments are not meant as a criticism of the Grantsman-ship Center's practices. It didn't invent the medical model; philanthropy did. Within that constraint, moreover, the center has helped a great many organizations and individuals do a better, more constructive job. The point is that the success of the center, and the fact that its recommendations can be recognized in so many proposals received by foundations and other funding sources today, shows that the center has had a good feel for what is effective in raising money.

Community organizations have a hard time using the Grantsman-ship Center format for applications. Other kinds of agencies may be able to talk in these terms, but it is difficult for community organizations. The realities of day-to-day community life just don't lend themselves to the confinement and social surgery suggested by the medical model. As Mary Ellen Montes of UNO says, "Everything ties together" all across a broad variety of interests and activities. Community organizations don't address one need at a time. Everything they do connects with everything else. Some of the best work is a spontaneous response to unpredictable events and opportunities, and precise objectives and methods usually evolve as the experience develops, as they did in MOP's work on the water supply contamination issue. It is very difficult to talk in terms of a schedule of specific and tangible achievements.

Worst of all among their difficulties with this proven formula for winning support, community organizations tend to question whether the medical model of philanthropy has worked all that well. Looking around their own communities, they see other types of agencies and institutions receiving support to solve piecemeal problems and the problems seem to outlast one grant after another. They doubt that community needs can be dealt with in this fashion.

There is nothing wrong with the medical model fundamentally. We need to fix things, and we certainly need to find "cures." The problem is with the way we get hooked by the model's appeal to our desire for convenient, tangible, and quick solutions to specific problems with which we feel comfortable. The ultimate medical model community groups can propose requires a sensitive audience that has not yet become common in philanthropy, and the cure they offer is the winning of a more active, participating citizenry, able to preserve and enrich our American democratic experience. Such a medical model may not have the simple attractions funding sources have traditionally looked for, but it's a model that deserves our attention today. Although it works on specific real issues in the community and is probably going to solve some tough community problems, the specific issues are always secondary to the overriding purpose. That's how the Adams County residents (chap. 5) were ready to move on from one very intensive activity to another; at least a partial cure had been won for the water supply, but in terms of an active citizen's vision of a proper community, that was just one step.

Judging by the three habits described here—giving to one's peers, funding institutional development and professional authority, and favoring proposals that promise sure and quick solutions to problems—people in philanthropy have behaved through the years the way pluralism scholars might predict. In a rational, economic fashion, we have found those patterns of giving with which we are comfortable and from which we get certain quid pro quo rewards. We generally feel better and gain more in return by giving to people with whom we can identify socially, either for their own benefit directly or for the good we believe they can do others. We enjoy playing an essential role in developing the American array of private not-for-profit institutions, governed by our peers and run by professionals, and we display on buildings and honor rolls the names of those who have made this private stewardship possible. And so that society may gain what seem the most measurable, dramatic satisfactions in return for our money, we prefer to choose for funding those opportunities that promise to isolate and address discrete problems that we are told can be efficiently solved through the investment of the grant requested.

To reflect even just this little on the history of these inclinations gives us some different insights about how they affect philanthropy:

- It seems odd today to have private philanthropy largely giving to those who are not poor. It becomes difficult to call it charity. We deal so often with only a partial and sometimes very small segment of our communities' population, and our intelligence and impact are severely limited. As an alternative choice, a deliberate focus on how philanthropy can be an enabling aid for poor people should make sense to more contributors.

- Support for the maintenance and growth of institutions and the professions is still at times a valid choice, but we are more aware today that such grants must be made selectively, and we know there is other philanthropic work to attend to, as well.

- The medical model has too often become a caricature of our liberal confidence that our sundry troubles can be licked if a few bright men and women of good spirit are given some grant money so they can isolate problems and apply their skills. We need philanthropists who are willing to say that the quest in real life is less surgical, more profound, and more rewarding. For the proper setting for that role, we turn to the subject of altruism.

CHAPTER 7

POLITICS AND ALTRUISM

Politics and altruism may seem strange bedfellows, but they have a revealing relationship when the subject is philanthropy and the support of community organizations.

Politics

Community organizations have no problem complying with the Internal Revenue Service requirements for charitable organizations. They don't campaign for candidates for office, and, just like other not-for-profit organizations, they can keep their legislative activity (lobbying) within the limits prescribed by law—limits that were clarified and liberalized by Congress in 1976. Yet a frequent foundation answer to community organization requests for funding is that the foundation "doesn't think it should get involved in politics." Meanwhile, the hospitals and major social service agencies that are being funded by the foundation are lobbying their socks off.

Actually, the activities of community organizations vis-à-vis local, state, and national legislative bodies are among the most appropriate for philanthropic support. Unlike hospitals, for instance, which find themselves embroiled in all sorts of legislative issues of crucial economic importance to them as institutions, community groups have no institutional self-interests to pursue. Their interests are directly citizen interests, arrived at deliberately among a significant body of citizens. If philanthropy literally means love of people, not love of institutions, that direct connection with the will of the community is attractive.

Outsiders with strong political inclinations sometimes look to community organizations for grass-roots confirmation of their own convictions. Politically progressive activists will suggest that community groups join in advocating a whole new American system with massive shifts of power. Politically conservative activists may try to overlay an organization's agenda with stern ideological concepts of law enforcement and welfare policy. But such doctrinaire people do a disservice to community groups when they try to impose their more exotic politics. Community organizations develop their own positions, ones that tend to have little to do with that world of parties, highly visible intramural fights, and the ideological arguments we are accustomed to think of as "politics," with headlines and television stories.

A specific experience provides an example. The Donors Forum of Chicago, one of our local "trade associations" in philanthropy, conducts trips to neighborhoods for its members. On one such trip, crime turned out to be a chief concern of the residents we were visiting. Afterwards, one of the Donors Forum members complained, "It was so hard to figure out where the people were coming from politically. . . . One moment they were talking about police brutality and the next moment they were calling for law and order and more police." Here was a good example of a community organization setting its own practical agenda. The residents wanted a law enforcement system that would work for them, and they knew from firsthand experience what was required: less fear of people being abused and more sense of visible, on-the-scene police readiness to protect the community. They couldn't care less about how their point of view squared with stereotypes of conservative and liberal or of one party versus another.

Bilingual education has been another area in which there has often been little connection between political rhetoric and the work of community groups. While others are using it as a political football and burdening the program with heroic, oversimplified positions pro and con, active parents groups in many communities take this additional resource at face value and try to make the most of it while they have it. They work with teachers, administrators, and children to see that bilingual education works in whatever ways possible to help their children get a better education, which certainly includes competence in English.

In any case, what a foundation is primarily investing in is not

the particular position the community group is taking, but rather
the process involved in reaching sound decisions and doing something about them. For the organization to be viable, there must
be priorities and goals and victories, and the foundation can certainly share in celebrating tangible gains achieved for the community. But for the foundation, the major interests and the most important returns on the grants it has made come from the process
itself: effective, broad-based participation; leadership that has
evolved; lessons that have been learned; and qualities that have
been established or refreshed in the public life of the community.

I don't mean to say that community organizing hasn't got anything to do with politics. On the contrary, it is a likely way for
people to get started on the road to becoming discriminating voters
who know what they and their communities need, vote accordingly, and hold accountable those whom they elect. As we saw in
the examples of BUILD, MOP, and UNO, community organization activity puts citizens in touch with larger arenas of discussion
and decision making. But what people carry into these larger arenas from participating in community groups is not doctrinaire politics learned from outside people and television, but a more pragmatic and humanistic view from a community vantage point based
on their own and their neighbors' experiences.

The two kinds of activity are not mutually exclusive. Lively political conversation in a community challenges a community organization to answer questions about its mission and its relevance
to various ideological positions that may be gaining community
attention. In turn, the community organization provides a forum—
"candidates' nights" are a common tradition—and often helps clarify
positions. At their most recent annual meeting, the members of
BUILD wrote a five-point "Municipal Agenda" of things they felt
needed to be attended to in the city, and then they used it to instruct the 1987 mayoral candidates. Perhaps most significantly, the
community organization, close to the ground and with a habit of
being skeptical, is the community's best guard against being swept
up by a demagogue of any persuasion.

Of course, there can be risks of embarrassment to foundations.
Communities are lively, unpredictable places, and the word *politics* can be applied to anything that happens that someone doesn't
like. But much more often, the community organizing process yields

acceptable, constructive results for right now and the promise of citizen competence that will be an important community asset for the future.

One foundation, which had made a relatively large grant to a community group in a Hispanic community, was about to have a board meeting at which a request from that group for renewed support was on the agenda. On the eve of the meeting, the foundation heard a report—through business and social connections—that the organization's employment committee, pressing a local company to hire Hispanics, had gone to see an executive of the company one evening at his home. The report said that the group had been rowdy, severely frightening the executive's family. The executive, who wasn't home at the time, was infuriated and saw to it that people connected with the organization's funding sources were notified of this breach of propriety. In the field of philanthropy where everyone on both sides of the equation is always so polite, this was very serious business.

The foundation in question deferred its decision about renewal and appointed a committee of three board members and the staff director to meet with representatives of both the company and the community group. The committee went to both places, asked questions, listened, and learned.

Although new directors were making the foundation board increasingly representative of the community, the board and its interviewing committee were (and most likely always would be) much closer culturally to the company executive and his beleaguered family than to the community group. The committee members sympathized with the members of the family who felt so threatened. But they found that although several police officers were on the scene throughout the incident, ready and willing to make arrests, no arrests were made. They also found that the company had not been receptive to more conventional requests for a meeting, and that, indeed, the personnel department's record of handling job applications from Hispanics was not impressive.

The company representatives with whom the committee met were friendly and sincere, but so were the men and women of the community organization—residents, volunteers, looking wherever they could for job opportunities for themselves, their families, and their neighbors.

The community organization kept pushing the company's top management for a meeting and the foundation for renewal of the grant. Ultimately, the foundation did renew the grant, and one of the company's officers did meet with the community group and accept some recommendations, including the appointment of a Hispanic to its personnel department.

It's a fairly modest story, and that's just the point. Most "conflict-of-interest" incidents in grants to community organizations boil down to circumstances like this. They happen very seldom, and when they do, troubles for funders and their friends are less any sort of hard economic threat and more a question of potential embarrassment among peers. These are surmountable situations that can be dealt with constructively if people so choose.

The episode is noteworthy in several respects. The members of the community organization kept their eyes on their objectives, neither giving in to pressures about funding nor losing their cool and getting angry at everybody. The company gave a little, and the executive and his family felt less intimidated as the relationship grew. The foundation, as one board member said later, "really didn't have to make a big judgment about who was right and who was wrong. . . . It wasn't a question of choosing sides. After all, the company wasn't asking for a grant." It was enough that the community organization was fulfilling a helpful, legitimate role in the community as an instrument for decent people to use in taking charge of their lives and addressing their own needs and issues in the best ways available to them—sometimes with confrontation, sometimes with methods less dramatic.

This hasn't really been a political story. The episode didn't involve any legislative positions or candidates, and neither the community group nor the company were eager to expand the situation and give it any larger meaning than it already had. But it seems to belong under "Politics" because it begins to get at a major question that remains: the politics of the foundation people and, perhaps, of the foundation itself.

I've suggested before that it can be difficult and inappropriate to match up a community organization's attitudes with one's own political stances on particular issues. But there's a more fundamental question than that, with which the foundation committee and board in our story struggled when they tried to reconcile their loyalties to both sides of the issue. Regardless of whether community organization members think about such things all the time (and I maintain they don't), in the foundation person's mind grants to community organizations *do* have political implications. You can go either way. From one standpoint, you are supporting processes that enable people without power to get some power, to begin establishing their own agenda, to begin asserting themselves, and to overcome exploitation and discrimination. Whether you figure your grant helps enable the group to fight the pluralist system or simply to join it, that grant takes a progressive position in favor of a more equitable distribution of power in America.

From another standpoint, however, you are supporting processes that are in the interests of the already established authorities in our society because community organizations are constructive alternatives to the threat of violence from those who see themselves hurting and wanting amid the riches of others. Community organizations civilize, they acculturate, they encourage orderliness. They provide firsthand early warning expressions of troubles. They are run not by do-gooders but by real people who seem more to be trusted. They may even help reduce dependency, welfare rolls, and taxes. A grant made with that rationale takes a conservative position.

How about a grant to UNO for organizing around the problem of the steel mills shutting down in southeast Chicago? Does that grant incite people to raise hell about the failure of the steel companies? Or does it encourage people to react to a potentially incendiary issue in a constructive, peaceful, rational fashion?

You can go either way, or in some other direction, in your own personal political interpretations of the value of such grants. So can each of the other board and staff members. You can even disagree on this general philosophical level while being of one mind about how the foundation should respond to the immediate situation. A.D. Lindsay, a respected American political philosopher in the first half of this century, remarked that "democracy is based on the assumption that men can agree on common action which yet leaves each to live his own life."

The foundation itself, however, really doesn't have to make this grand choice about ultimate political implications. It meets the community organization members where they are and takes their agenda at face value. That agenda is to realize the American Dream. No one shows more desire to reach for that dream than the poor people in the community organizations of the cities and rural areas of this country. The foundation, impressed with their potential, responds.

Altruism

So if it's not an opportunity to pursue one's own political inclinations, what is the motivation for making grants to community organizations? The answer that such grants enhance democratic participation is fine, but it barely digs into what's really going on in the experience and attitudes of the giver.

First, it's necessary to look more generally at what constitutes altruism, at least in the context of giving away money. There's a good deal of fresh interest in altruistic behavior. We are told that psychologists are tending to look more at the positive aspects of how we act toward one another; *prosocial* behavior is a relatively new and frequent term that seems synonymous with altruism. There is also the startling new field of sociobiology, in which biologists and some social scientists are leading the way in taking the principles and learnings of evolutionary theory and applying them in a more lively fashion than before to questions of animal and human behavior, including questions about altruism.

In its purest state, altruism refers to an act that is "socially valuable but individually disadvantageous." It seems generally agreed, however, that in real life there are rewards to the giver of one kind or another, so that altruism involves benefits to the recipient, costs to the donor, and gains for the donor. If the costs of an act of altruism truly outweigh the donor's gains, then it is indeed "individually disadvantageous." If the gains outweigh the costs, the act shouldn't qualify as altruism. At least that's a useful way to approach the subject, even if it soon refuses to stay put within such a neat and tidy equation.

Just a few comments about the first two ingredients above and then a little more than that about the third. I realize this sounds like the beginning of a whole new book; I promise it won't be. But why we give money away is a good, rewarding question that never gets the respect it deserves in philanthropy, and it has some special implications when we're talking about grants to community organizations.

Benefits to the Recipient

I propose three arbitrary assumptions. First, "recipients" of philanthropy ultimately has to mean real people out there in the public, not schools or hospitals or other institutions or their employees. We are too often comfortable with the simple elite partnership of us and the institutions and professionals we support, as though we and they were the whole give-and-take universe of philanthropy. We and they are not. There can be other considerations—in support for artists, for instance—but by and large the importance of our grants lies in what they do for the public.

Second, there must truly be net benefits to those recipients for an act to qualify as altruistic. The foundation may feel generous in doing what it does, but in our real world of scarce resources, urgent needs, and people hurting, good intentions are not enough. If the grant turns sour and is wasted, if the benefits never reach the intended people, or if the funded program does more harm than good, it isn't altruistic.

And third, a philanthropic gift should be something welcome and nurturing to the ultimate recipients. The record of unpopular charity "done for their own good" is not good. That assumption can have its difficulties, but it's better to start with it than with the all too frequent operating principle that the funding source and its agents know more about what's good for people than the people do.

These considerations about benefits to the recipients of altruism are useful here mostly as a brief complement to what follows. But it's worth noting that they are especially well realized in grants to community organizations—grants made directly to groups of community people for current work important to them.

Costs to the Donor

When an individual contributes money to a favorite charity, the costs, if any, are fairly easy to identify. Foundations are more complicated. First, there is the capital involved in setting up the foundation. For some philanthropists this may represent no cost at all in terms of sacrifice; to use Eduard Lindeman's term, it was truly surplus funds. However, for others—more than may usually be assumed—there are significant costs. Even with tax advantages, many donors to foundations and their children and children's children live different lifestyles than they would have if the money hadn't been given away. To an outsider these differences may seem painless, but in the lives of the donors and their families they are meaningful cost considerations in establishing foundations.

Not only is the money taken away from the donors' unrestricted personal use, but the donors also give up control of its philanthropic use, giving that prerogative to a board of directors. Even if they prescribe in the incorporation papers that the money be used in very specific ways, they lose the power to change that focus in the future. That's a cost.

Second, donors and board members give time and effort to foundation affairs. The amount of this cost varies greatly, but again I suspect common prejudices underestimate actual conditions. Anyone who has seen the quantity and complexity of homework required before a board meeting of a foundation that has active directors, or anyone who has been to one of those difficult special meetings where the agenda is to adopt or refresh goals and priorities, knows that the task of governing a foundation can be hard, frustrating, demanding work.

Third, for any given grant, there is the cost of not being able to fund other proposals. To the donor or board member who has other favorite causes for which grants would be especially satisfying and perhaps more personally advantageous, that's a cost that often lingers on in the life of a grant, daring it to fail.

Finally, in an often hostile or at least skeptical public environment, there are personal risks involved—embarrassment when supported programs go awry, criticism when other people don't like what's being funded, bitterness among those turned down. These risks are also costs, as are the risks of personal disappointment, discouragement, and disillusionment, and there can be plenty of these.

I am not looking for sympathy. Indeed, I think foundation people get it all back and more. But it's important to establish that there are costs. "Give till it hurts" may not be a day-to-day operative principle in foundation work, but the costs are sufficient to allow us to say that there is a transaction of sorts, in which something of value is given up and others benefit.

Gains for the Donor
There are also rewards for the altruist, in this case the philanthropist. To quote psychologist Derek Wright:

> It does not follow that altruistic actions have no beneficial consequences for the actor. On the contrary, they are bound to have some consequences. . . . But the rewarding consequences for the individual may not be obvious, and the forms they take are often subtle and obscure.

Before concentrating on those gains that are "subtle and obscure," perhaps we can get money out of the way. Some foundations pay a fee to their board members, including donors, just like directors' fees in business corporations. There can be good reasons for doing so, including the development of boards that are more representative of the community; some members cannot so easily afford to volunteer. But with a few exceptions, the amount given is a small honorarium, not much compared with time and effort given.

I'm also going to minimize the significance of business and social benefits that come from giving. Given the type of grants this book is about, there is limited potential. One just doesn't get many immediate business and social benefits from supporting a community organization in a poor community compared with the potential fallout from a grant to a major museum, university, or hospital. That doesn't mean there can't be more profound consequences for one's public position because, of course, there can. But there isn't the quid pro quo here that some donors especially look for.

So, then, the more relevant, less material gains to which Derek Wright refers can be summarized under five headings:

- *Self-realization.* Those active in foundation work confirm what an unusual personal opportunity this is. The board members described earlier, who were concerned observers in the relationship between a community organization and a corporate employer, emerged from that experience different from when they went in. As they all said, it was a stretching, growing experience, important in the lives of the foundation people as well as the organization members and corporate representatives. Any altruistic act can produce a certain euphoria; experiences like this one, with a broad variety of people in a community context, provide something more lasting. These board members were able to "recognize the other person's reality," as Thomas Nagel says. And to cite Nagel further regarding the utility of such an encounter to the giver, "It is a question not of compassion but of simply connecting, in order to see what one's attitudes commit to." You learn about yourself, apply what you learn, and learn again. That's the best of education, in terms that call to mind John Dewey's convictions. Participating in the community activities of a democratic society, including its philanthropy, is indeed "a life of free and enriching communion."

Hannah Arendt's evocative comments in *The Human Condition* reflect on the value of that kind of experience and how rare it is today. She says our time is dominated by our *private* lives and *social* lives, both of which we pursue to meet personal "maintenance" needs. The Greeks, about whom she is writing, prized their chances to have also a "common public life," in which they might talk with others, work out differences, and meet the needs and opportunities of community. Participating in "the world that is common to us" was the way they felt they realized their full worth as individual human beings—freely, nonviolently, politically.

In a different era when we may not always recognize our chances to be so civilized, foundation people making grants to community organizations find their work brings them in touch with public life in a way that is not showy and conspicuous but very rewarding, whether one then chooses to become more directly involved or not.

- *The satisfaction of meeting moral responsibilities.* Immanuel Kant presented the moral case for altruism in 1797, in no uncertain terms:

> To help other men according to our ability is a duty, whether we love them or not; and even if it turns out the human species, on closer acquaintance, does not

seem particularly lovable, this would not detract from
the force of our duty to help others.

The second half of the statement is more than an after-
thought. Kant considered the task of meeting one's moral
obligations in helping others to be more important than
any imperative to love. He believed the capacity to love
comes from successfully addressing the first task: "If a
man practices it [helping others] often and succeeds in
realizing his purpose, he eventually comes to feel love for
those he has helped. Hence the saying: you *ought* to love
your neighbor means *do good* to your fellowman and this
will give rise to love."

We are most apt to identify our cultural traditions of altruism with religion. All the world's religions have in common a basic principle of helping others in need. The Old
Testament instructions in Deuteronomy 15:7–11 conclude,
"You shall open wide your hand to your brother, to the
needy and to the poor, in the land." In the culmination of
Jesus' teaching ministry—his last words in the temple at
Jerusalem—he built upon the law of Deuteronomy and proposed a dramatic conversation with his people:

Then the King will say to those at his right hand,
"Come, O blessed of my Father, inherit the kingdom
prepared for you from the foundation of the world;
for I was hungry and you gave me food,
I was thirsty and you gave me drink,
I was a stranger and you welcomed me,
I was naked and you clothed me,
I was sick and you visited me,
I was in prison and you came to me."
Then the righteous will answer him,
"Lord, when did we see thee hungry and feed thee,
      or thirsty and give thee drink?
And when did we see thee a stranger and welcome
      thee, or naked and clothe thee?
And when did we see thee sick or in prison and visit
      thee?"
And the King will answer them, "Truly, I say to you,

as you did it to one of the least of these my
brethren, you did it to me."
                                    (Matthew 25:34–40)

A purist may deny that there can be gain from the ful-
fillment of moral responsibilities. Virtue is its own reward.
But there has always been the promise of other benefits.
Virtue is rewarded. Kant speaks of the satisfaction a rich
man derives from his beneficence. And one of the great
songs of the later Isaiah asks that we be good-hearted and
help the oppressed, promising,

if you pour yourself out for the hungry
    and satisfy the desire of the afflicted,
then shall your light rise in the darkness
    and your gloom be as the noonday.
                                    (Isaiah 58:10)

In the Bible, then, there is a consistent relationship between the God-like act of selflessness and an acceptance
of the fact that giving will help us now or later or both.
After Christ's message in Jerusalem that the blessed
altruists will inherit the kingdom prepared for them, he
continues to say that those who do not help others in need
will be told, "Depart from me, you cursed, into the eter-
nal fire prepared for the devil and his angels" (Matthew
25:41). Faced with options such as these, it should not be
difficult for us to determine where our self-interests lie.

Despite the presumptions of our secular, pro-rational society, philanthropy still has at its roots in our culture a
strong connection with these concepts of moral responsibilities and motivations. A foundation provides an appropriate vehicle for giving to philanthropy a sense of purpose,
order, and achievement that will help people meet the
responsibilities they feel.

There are parallels between how people in philanthropy can act upon their moral convictions and how the leaders
quoted in chapter 5 regard their experiences with community organizations. These organizations, like the foundations, become vehicles. "The community became the

place where we could act out our faith together," as Vicki
Ceja says.

- *Esteem.* Philanthropy has always been a high road to public esteem. In our American experience, we impute to most
  of our philanthropists a generosity that strengthens our
  regard for them. We accept the fact that the winning of
  esteem is one reason they do what they do. We judge their
  wishes to be well remembered as being a proper part of
  their motivations for giving.

  Recognition in philanthropy has changed some in the
  past twenty-five years. Especially with the growth of local, regional, and national associations in the foundation
  field, there are more reference points for donors, board
  members, and staffs, more places where a foundation person first becomes known as a peer among foundation people and then is recognized among an extended public of
  others with whom the associations relate. Certainly not
  all foundation people choose to involve themselves in these
  relationships, but the fruits of their labors become better
  known today, in any case. IRS requirements and a general
  move toward openness today make for a broader and more
  accurate public knowledge of philanthropic programs. And
  as that public knowledge grows, it becomes more discriminating. Giving programs that seem to offer refreshing new help and hope for the community are noticed and
  appreciated.

- *Reciprocity.* There are several possible points of entry into
  philanthropy from the perspectives of sociobiology. The
  one that seems most appropriate is reciprocity, the inclination we and most animals have to trade favors with one
  another. Cooperation is part of it, but that usually means
  people working together at the same overall task at the same
  time. In reciprocity, our acts may be very different and
  spaced so far apart in time and context as to be hard to
  assemble into a pair. French politician and writer Alexis
  de Toqueville speaks of reciprocity in his famous work,
  Democracy in America, when he considers our emerging
  American habits:

> Equality of condition [in pioneer America], while it
> makes men feel their independence, shows them their
> own weakness; they are free but exposed to a thou-
> sand accidents; and experience soon teaches them that
> although they do not habitually require the assistance
> of others, a time almost always comes when they can-
> not do without it.

Biologists and anthropologists, studying our genes and cul-
tures, agree that Americans, along with everybody else,
"cannot do without" helpful experiences with others. We
participate not only in the more visible "You scratch my
back, I'll scratch yours" exchanges reminiscent of the
pluralist bargaining and economic model discussed in chapter 2, but also in countless unspoken and unarticulated contracts of which we may be either unaware or only dimly
aware.

We learn two things especially from these new perspectives. First is the importance of future generations when
considering reciprocity. Sociobiologists are mostly interested in what we do for our kin. If they were to concentrate some attention on foundations, they would very likely
make a valid evolutionary case for grants to organizations
whose work can help make life safer and more enjoyable
in the communities in which the families of foundation people, their children and children's children, their nieces and
nephews and cousins may live in the future. The biological argument is that those grants are attractive because they
are genetically advantageous; they are likely to contribute
to reproductive success. In these days when children grow
up and move all over the place, we may need to change
the rules and figure we are taking care of some other
donor's gene pool while he or she takes care of ours, but
that just adds an additional layer of reciprocity. The principle still holds.

It is therefore profoundly natural for a philanthropist to
make grants to organizations that seek to enhance the quality and security of public life, develop community leadership, and address basic concerns such as school systems

and toxic wastes. It becomes very easy to feel the sense of reciprocity between donors and community organizations when you support groups such as BUILD, MOP, and UNO.

Sociobiologists aren't the only ones who feel a sense of urgency in helping us think clearly about our responsibilities to the future. In a hard-nosed, unsentimental collection of articles called *Obligations to Future Generations*, sociologist Brian Barry concludes with an argument that is familiar to most people of wealth who have decided on a course of philanthropy. It is not enough to provide for one's own children alone, he says, because

> the welfare of individual members of the next generation is interdependent. Even if I do the best I can for those members of the next generation in whose welfare I have some psychic investment, the main determinant of their future prospects is the kind of world that they will live in, and that depends overwhelmingly on the decisions of others.

> The welfare of the next generation is thus a public good. If I want my children to have a better public park, I have to be prepared to pay my share; and the same goes if I want them to have a better world.

The emphasis on future generations is useful because it encourages a longer view of lives ahead to go alongside our more common and equally valid attention to what's going on right now. Who are the people who will someday benefit from the present work of BUILD, MOP, and UNO in so many different ways, and what will their relationships be like together in larger communities? Perhaps part of the foundation person's role as an altruist is to seek reciprocity for his or her grants with future generations, and in the process be more aware of the longer-term implications of what happens today.

The second thing we learn from sociobiologists is how altruism affects community. In the new *Journal of Social and Biological Structures*, Shmuel Amir and David Bigman look for "the reason behind altruism":

> [A]ltruism survives because it enhances community cohesiveness and because its benefits to the individual are inextricably connected to the emergence and development of vigorous and prosperous communities. . . .

> Altruistic behavior, which manifests one's care for the interest of the community, is more than compensated for by the rewards gained by belonging to the community.

Writing as an anthropologist, Ronald Cohen says much the same thing: "The presence and persistence of altruistic values or elements of altruism have survival value for the group that maintains such beliefs."

The philanthropists practicing altruism in communities, as well as their families and friends, are served by this survival value along with everyone else. In the interests of reciprocity they look for opportunities to contribute to a community that will be a good place for everybody, a community that has arrangements most conducive to letting its citizens live lives fulfilled.

Thinking in terms like these, of course, one loses all track of who helps whom. Everybody wins, there is joy all around, and the divisions of costs and gains we began with turns out to be a mean and inadequate little device.

• *Pleasures.* There are pleasures in altruism, I'm sure. But in this catalog of philanthropic motivations, I'd like to include one satisfaction that can coexist with altruism and be its turning wheel but is still something different. Here is the foundation person as entrepreneur, a capitalist who enjoys collecting not money but equity investments in constructive community activity.

I once wrote an irreverent column about a favorite fantasy: suppose there were a market, like a stock market, where foundation people traded among themselves the grants they had made. Some grants would sell high—higher than the original amount given to the grantee—when the activity funded appeared to be headed for success. Other grants would sell lower than their original face value when things weren't looking so good.

If a foundation felt that a grant some other foundation had made was selling lower than its real value—that is, the activity supported had some unrecognized potential that might be realized—it would buy the grant. If a foundation felt that one of its own grants was in trouble, it might try to sell the grant before the price went down.

At the end of each day, a widely disseminated *Foundation News* computer printout would show the day's market value of each grant and its gain or loss for the day. More than that, it would also add up the total market value of all grants currently belonging to each foundation and arrive at a "foundation performance index" (FPI) of how that total compared with the original face value of the grants made by the foundation. Every foundation staff and board person would have a daily display of how the foundation's current grant portfolio was doing, how the grants it had sold to others were doing, and how its FPI compared with others. The daily comparative FPIs, of course, would make interesting reading for lots of other people, too.

Some growth-oriented foundations would specialize in picking up bargain grants from other foundations and trying to nurse them back into higher-quality holdings. Others would only deal in blue chips, keeping their own best grants and buying other people's with proceeds from the sales of their mistakes.

There would be special awards for the top performers, presented at the annual Council on Foundations conference. In the case of those unfortunate others at the bottom of the list, the foundation field has always been looking for a way to police itself, and low FPIs are the answer we've all been waiting for.

There are all kinds of possibilities. The foundation that made a grant in the first place could always buy it back at the original value plus 15 percent, with the stipulation that it couldn't sell the grant again for eight months. Good grants could come home again, and there would finally be a chance to answer in practice rather than theory that grand old classic foundation question: would you buy the grant back if you had the chance?

Alas, we don't have a grants market yet. But even without one, good foundation people think of their grants as port- folios. Those grants they made last month aren't just cash kissed away; they are investments made, which need to be followed, helped, evaluated, fixed, and pushed into becom- ing top performers. Otherwise, the foundation's FPI will go down, and if it does, watch out.

Someday I'm going to turn this fantasy into a game foun- dation people can play, like Monopoly. Players would represent different foundations and compete for success in their grant portfolios. I like it because it emphasizes the process of making grants and following through on them, a process that is exciting and rewarding in itself when it's well pursued.

Such pleasures don't jeopardize the altruism involved. A morally right act doesn't become less creditable because its performance gives one satisfaction. Quite to the con- trary, it's a good thing when the sentiments involved in philanthropic giving and getting aren't limited to self- sacrifice on one side and gratitude on the other. There can then be fewer risks of the donee feeling the counterproduc- tive burdens of obligation. Both sides can be steadier in their realization that their real responsibilities are to the community. Maybe my game should have a couple of characters who are heads of community organizations, struggling not with the task of being grateful but rather with the heavy load of being expected to save the world for the grantor's grandchildren.

Further, the activity dramatized by the game is appropri- ate to philanthropic altruism because it is a never-ending experience. There's always another grant to add to the roll- ing total. In evolutionary terms, single games never pay off. Reciprocity takes time and renewal. As the sociobiol- ogists say: "In the language of game theory, the altruist considers life as a recurring game to be played at each ins- tant with no need, at least in principle, to come to an end."

The grants that lie at the center of these altruistic considerations are those to community organizations. Enabling a community to find its "common public life" seems to promote the best kind of *self-realization* in philanthropy. Helping poor people identify and solve their own problems and win respect must be among the longest, steadiest strides in *meeting one's moral responsibilities*. The good sense of supporting community groups as a first-class investment in democracy garners *esteem* in the modern world of philanthropy. There is no more appropriate way to initiate *reciprocity* with present and future generations of community people than making grants to the organizations they themselves create to press for improvements in the quality of life in their communities. And the grants market game runs best and yields the most *pleasure* when the action is close by and the grants are not to institutions but go directly to community people.

Politics and altruism are in the same chapter so I can make the point that when foundation people support community organizations, they are being not politicians but altruists. There are lots of other opportunities to be political, such as grants to agents of specific causes, or grants to agencies and institutions whose causes may not be explicit but whose leaders are known for partisan views which, one way or another, become expressed in the institution's impact on society. In such instances, foundations are joining with their grantees in trying to advance their positions on specific political issues. Such grants are not to be condemned, at least not here, but need to be recognized for what they are: political.

When foundations support community organizations, on the other hand, the grants are not to issues but to communities. The foundations are not imposing on the communities their own political ideologies or their favorite solutions to community problems. Nor are they imposing the ideologies and favorite solutions of professional friends. The grants are nonmanipulative, nonpower seeking. The foundations gain the satisfaction of being useful to people within the contexts of the people's own identities, not the foundation's. The organizations and their funded activities belong to the citizens to work with and grow with.

It's a paradox. In these grants that have so much to do with public life, the prime business of philanthropy turns out to be not politics but altruism. That's why a foundation program supporting community organizations, compared with a lot of other fields of philanthropy, seems to have an irrefutable, unassailable basic usefulness.

CHAPTER 8

HOW TO EVALUATE PROPOSALS FROM COMMUNITY ORGANIZATIONS

It seems time now to move to a more nuts-and-bolts topic. For better or worse, the conventional procedure of philanthropy is to base grant decisions on written proposals. Some people think that's ridiculous, that the development of a good trusting relationship transcends what can be put on paper; proposals are just ceremonies, they say.

Maybe. There certainly can be good conversations. But ultimately it's useful to both the donee and donor to have some crucial points expressed as clearly as possible in writing. What that proposal can say sums up the understanding everyone has when a grant is made. Whether a formal document or a short informal letter, it can get both sides ready to move ahead. The following discussion, therefore, assumes that the most important elements of a community organization's proposal to a potential contributor will be committed to writing.

Four Working Criteria

Four criteria have been especially helpful in evaluating proposals from community organizations. They are presented here, accompanied by questions that seem to lead to useful information. Some of the answers should be in the proposal itself, some can be in a handy basic fact sheet about the organization, and some may be in a follow-up letter you can ask for. Other answers, regardless of the value of written material, you will get informally, orally. Still other answers are obviously opinions you develop yourself as you see what's going on. And still others are answers you will never get just because no one can ever ask all the right questions.

The principles on which these criteria are based are the same as those presented in the specifications of chapter 4. But now it's a question of whether community organizations can show that they are building the *strengths*, developing the *functions*, and having the *results* spelled out in those considerations.

Some of the questions will bring to mind information in the descriptions of BUILD, MOP, and UNO, three community organizations that could answer virtually all the questions posed here with relative ease. Newer or less-developed organizations can't be expected to give complete answers to a lot of the questions. That shouldn't disqualify them; putting a community organization together takes a while and it's an important, lively time well worth supporting. But there should be indications that they are moving toward the criteria suggested here.

These are mostly questions just between you and the organization itself. You may very likely know other people with different types of organizations nearby, and it's certainly good to ask around. But community organizations are different enough from social service agencies and other organizations to deserve an independent appraisal.

For some questions here, you either have to carry out independent inquiries or accept the organization's information just as you do with other grantees. Successful grants do require building a mutual trust. Most community organizations will respect your interest in asking for specific facts and figures. They will also respect the way you check with others in the community.

Legitimacy in the Community

It is important to find out if the organization is designed in such a way that it can have a solid position in the community, and then whether it is winning that position.

1. Is the structure of the organization clear?
   * Who is supposed to belong? Are the members churches, neighborhood groups, block clubs and other organizations and institutions, or individuals, or both? What does it take to become a member?
   * Are there geographic boundaries?

- Who runs it? Is there a board, a leadership council, a senate, committees?
- Is there an annual convention at which the membership determines directions and elects membership?
- Are there bylaws that spell out these arrangements?

2. Is there evidence that the organization is the same in real life as it is on paper?
   - Who actually belongs? Is there a list of current members—institutions and organizations and their leaders, or individuals, or both?
   - Is there financial and in-kind support from some of the members or from the community generally (through fund raisers, for instance)?
   - Who's on the board? Who are the officers? Is there a list of board members with addresses and perhaps their other affiliations and community experience?
   - How many people came to the most recent annual convention? Did they come as representatives of organizations? Or as individuals? What did they do at the convention? Did they hold elections? Set priorities?

3. What other significant organizations and institutions are there in the community? What relationships does this organization have with them?
   - Do some of those other organizations belong to this one, or at least work with it?
   - Are the leaders of this one active in some of the others?
   - On the other hand, is this organization independent of political, business, or institutional control so it can be trusted by community people as belonging to them?

Competence

Community organizations need to show competence in both organizing activity and administration. Training programs become essential ways of developing that competence among leaders and staff.

1. Organizing activity:
   - Does the organization seem able to bring significant numbers of people together to work on shared concerns? In such work, are they identifying community interests clearly?
   - Do they keep good track of people, especially new people? For instance, do they always have sign-up sheets at meetings? If so, how do they follow up with newcomers?
   - Are they capable and creative in finding out what they need to know and in formulating ideas for solving problems and moving ahead?
   - Are they able to assign responsibilities for leadership in carrying out plans, and do those who accept such responsibilities follow through?
   - What relationships does the organization have with the community's elected representatives? Does its activities help people become more politically aware and competent?
   - What specific accomplishments can they show that have helped the community? Are these achievements victories for only a few people or do they at least begin to involve and benefit the community as a whole?
   - What have they learned from their experiences?

2. Administrative: Although everyone should try to keep a community organization as unbureaucratic as possible, there are the same essentials you look for in other potential grantees.
   - Do they have an orderly bookkeeping system, adequate financial reports, and a certified annual audit? Do they comply with federal and state government reporting requirements applicable to not-for-profit corporations?
   - Are there clear policies about relationships between board and staff, hiring and firing, pay, insurance, etc.?
   - Are they able to raise some money in the community and from their church denominations or other close contacts?

Community organizations in poor communities don't have

the funds for sophisticated administrative systems that many other not-for-profits do, but there need to be these basic provisions and an attitude of administrative responsibility.

Annual certified audits seem especially important, not so much to discourage any deliberate impropriety but rather for their usefulness in counteracting a common tendency about priorities. Too many valuable community organizations have failed because in the midst of putting together great community campaigns, no one was paying enough attention to the formalities of accounting. After a while it gets to be too late to do anything about it. Some arbitrary rules seem in order for both your sake and that of the organization. For instance, consider a policy that says all proposals must have attached to them a satisfactory audit by a certified public accountant covering the previous fiscal year if that year ended longer than seven months ago, or covering the fiscal year previous to that one if the most recent year ended less than seven months ago. (If the latter, there needs to be evidence that a new audit will be available soon.) Exceptions need to be made for new organizations; see "Internal Revenue Service Status" below.

3. Training:
   - Is there a plan, written down, for training activities to add to the skills and insights of the membership as a whole and the leaders and staff? Is there evidence that the plan is being carried out effectively? Does it reach out to those who will be future leaders?
   - Does the training program build loyalty to the organization?

Focus

A community organization is faced with all of life in its community. That's part of its uniqueness; it has the whole vigor of community experience to work from. Yet it can't do everything at once, and that's a dilemma. Somehow, without losing the lively perspective of a holistic reflection of community, it has to carve out pieces to work on. That needs to be a deliberate focusing process run by the people who live in the community.

1. Is there a system whereby community people express their concerns about what's happening in the community and then choose what set of needs and opportunities the community organization is going to focus on during, for instance, the coming year?

2. In this process, does it seem that the members have a chance to grow in their understanding of what the issues are?

Participation and Leadership Development

Good organizing means constantly recruiting and encouraging people to become involved, to take a stand, to enjoy the process, and—for some—to grow into positions of leadership. It won't involve everybody; many will never join at all, and many others will join in only around a limited set of interests. But the whole proof of the organization's value has to be in how a significant number of people participate in the work and in how a continuous flow of new leadership for the community is generated by the process.

1. Again, how many people participated in the most recent annual convention? What parts of the community did they come from? Were they representative of the community?

2. Who got elected to be board members and officers? What parts of the community are *they* from? Are some of them reelected, some new?

3. What's the membership like of committees working on two or three of the major activities chosen for current focus? How many people? How did they get there? Who's in charge?

4. Do the staff and top leaders serve as facilitators—encouraging and enabling members of committees, for instance, to take responsibility for assembling information, getting in touch with other people, and deciding what to do and doing it? Or do a few leaders and staff assume the role of experts on everything, expecting the membership to follow?

5. Do the staff and leadership help members get better or-

ganized in their own local churches, block clubs, agencies, etc., so they can strengthen their own organizations and address their own institutional and neighborhood problems?

6. Are there experiences that cultivate relationships with people from other communities, other kinds of backgrounds?

7. Is there a list of some people who have come up in the organization and become leaders in the community, not only in this organization but in other roles as well? Is it an old list or does it look as though this is a lively process going on right now?

I believe these criteria are useful. I couldn't evaluate a proposal from a community organization without them. But just as parts of the descriptions of BUILD, MOP, and UNO probably make a community organization's work sound too easy, I worry about how a reader may overreact to the orderliness of these criteria and assume that community organizations can always be rational and predictable.

Community life doesn't permit such luxuries. It isn't homogeneous enough and it won't stand still. Impacts are often indirect; the best anticrime program turns out to be the organizing of block clubs and other associations, not necessarily around the issue of crime specifically, but around whatever interests people have, just because a community of less-isolated people is less vulnerable. That's why it is so important to keep one's eye steady on the fourth item, "Participation and Leadership Development," more than on the others; no matter what unpredictable things happen to the community, no matter how plans have to be changed, one can see how the organizing experience gives something of value to a significant number of people. The Adams County, Colo., members of MOP and their staff passed the test. They became deeply involved in an unpredicted major issue with lots of television and other excitement; yet when it was all over, they were able to celebrate what they had accomplished, learn from the experience, and be that much more useful to their communities as they moved on to other concerns.

This is a field where process is so important for both the community organization and the contributor. What counts is not just what specific near-term objectives the organization wants to achieve, but also how it gets there and what its constituents gain from the experience. Victories are important, but as John Simon says about philanthropy itself, it's not a question of whether the game is worth the candle; "the game *is* the candle." The lasting worth of community organization activities and the contributions that support them are what these processes mean to community people. As Ms. Ceja said after a MOP organizing experience, people in the neighborhood now "know they have something to work for. They know they can use their own strengths and resources."

Then there is one more question: do the community organization and the funding source share a sense of values? The previous chapter talked about how a potential contributor approaches a community organization in a nonpartisan, nonpolitical fashion, and that's still true. But beyond or beneath those considerations, the contributor needs to feel that this group's goals and habits are a good match with his or her own values. As with lots of other relationships in life, one can't always be 100 percent sure of that match on the first date, but it shouldn't take too long.

If you rebel at the detail of my criteria and demand that I boil it all down to a few basic requirements to look for in a community organization, I can pick just five key points: (1) laypeople of the community—volunteers—have to be in charge, not staff or one or two egocentric leaders; (2) a significant number of people must be involved who are typical of the community (what a "significant number" is depends on the situation, but the group must either have credibility now as an important community forum, voice, and action arm or have a strong potential for gaining that credibility); (3) there must be some clear immediate objectives based on thoughtful identification of needs, and at least some initial progress in using intelligence from inside and outside the community to formulate strategies and plans to meet those objectives; (4) a decent system must be in place for handling money and accounting for it; and (5) a deliberate, active training program for leaders, future leaders, and staff is essential.

Choices: Either. . .Or

Much that is left is a matter of judgment. Here are five choices one can make in funding community organizations. Again, the considerations hark back to the characteristics needed for enhancing participation (chap. 4).

General Operating Support Versus Project Funding
There is a trade-off. Especially if the donor is new to the field, there is something to be said for grants to specific projects or fields of interest *provided that* (1) an ample amount is built into each grant for administrative supervision and overhead, and (2) the project isn't off on some sidetrack but rather is an important part of the organization's mandated organizing activity. This gets close to the medical model of philanthropy, with all its promise and hazards. When you fund specific work of the organization in, let's say, helping a group of its constituents who are welfare recipients get involved in current efforts to reform welfare policies, the "contract" between the organization and the donor is clear, the goals are as explicit as the unpredictability of community life will allow, and it's easier to watch and learn from the experience. You still have to know something about the organization as a whole, but it's easier.

On the other hand, project funding involves the danger of suggesting that work on specific, predetermined issues is more important than building participation and leadership in activities across a broader range of community concerns. General operating support shows more understanding of the value of both. It also underscores the fact that the community organization, not the funding source, is responsible for choosing priorities, setting objectives, and establishing strategies. And it shows appreciation for the way in which a community organization has to be ready to respond to new concerns in the community and be creative in ways that can't be anticipated.

The choice has to be worked out between donor and donee. If a specific field or project is chosen, however, the proposal should place as much emphasis on the organizing process and its rewards as it does on the specific improvements the organization wants to achieve in welfare policies, jobs, housing, schools, or whatever the project is concerned with. It should also summarize, briefly, the other work the community organization is doing and answer the general organizational questions about structure and procedure contained in the four criteria listed above.

Large Organizations Versus Small Ones

It's easy to be attracted to a large community organization covering a substantial geographic area. It seems more significant. But economist Mancur Olson and others have given us strong arguments in favor of smaller groups. Smaller groups have an easier time maintaining a satisfactory level of participation, with people feeling they have a voice in the organization and something to gain from joining in. Big organizations carry the danger of more free riders, who just assume others will take care of business for them. So if an organization is large, it's important to see that it is made up of active smaller groups and that a deliberate effort is made to make participation meaningful to the broadest possible range of people. BUILD and MOP cover big areas; the comments of their leaders show how important they feel it is to keep attention focused on the various neighborhood components. UNO of South East Chicago is part of a larger group, UNO of Chicago, but it is firm in its determination not only to retain its own autonomy but also to respect the identity of the several neighborhoods that make up its own membership.

Long-Term Versus Short-Term Support

This is a familiar philanthropic puzzle. Despite the need for periodic reports and refreshed applications, community organizations seem good candidates for more consistent support than they usually get. It's easy to see a double standard at work sometimes: major cultural institutions, for instance, get support year in and year out with little argument, but community organizations have hard times getting multiyear grants or one-year grants renewed.

Most worthwhile activities addressing major community issues take a while. Usually, the more important the problems are, the less realistic it is to expect them to be solved in a year or two or three. The basic tasks—building participation and leadership, strengthening the community—are continuing ones year after year. New issues manifest themselves, new leadership evolves. A vigorous

community organization should be able to make it clear that neither
the actions of the organization nor the investments of its contributors are in a rut. It should also be able to show persistent efforts
to raise funds elsewhere, even though it becomes evident that other
sources may indeed be limited.

Established Organizations Versus New Ones

At the same time, with community organizations that have been
around awhile, it is especially important to check whether the activity and leadership achievements are current. There can be laurels
being rested on, old victories being relived, veteran leaders who
no longer have the position in the community they used to have.

In an established organization, what's been learned? How successful have they been in maintaining a flow of new leadership?
The lives of community organizations can reveal cycles: after a
great productive period, perhaps fatigue sets in, leaders and staff
move on, or maybe an important person dramatically defects or
"sells out" under pressure. Momentum and loyalty are lost, and
the essential regeneration of leadership slows way down. Sometimes it is important to help an organization survive a transition
period when not much is happening, but eventually a judgment
has to be made: what signs are there that the organization will get
reinvigorated?

One needs to value the track record and sophistication of established organizations. In comparison, new organizations may not
have everything put together yet, but they can have a fresh enthusiasm and a feeling of ownership among their members that make
them especially effective and valuable to their communities.

Big Issues Versus Little Ones

It's always good to find an organization that is addressing a set
of highly sophisticated issues creatively and forcefully. But if that's
all there is, there have to be suspicions. A lively organization requires that new people become involved all the time, and it's likely
their initial activities will be around immediate problems closest
to home. For the early progress of people becoming active citizens,
issues such as garbage service, heat, stop signs, local school-
community relations, and police patrols have always been more
crucial than more complicated ones. If no one is working on those,

the organization's constituency may be very thin.

Multi- Versus Single-Interest Organizations

There are a lot of single-interest citizens organizations, created by groups of people across the city or the state or whatever who are interested in better schools, more jobs, or some other concern. They are very different from multi-interest community organizations in specific communities. It's usually the multi-interest community organization that does most of the basic organizing and training, helping people define and pursue whatever they want to work on. A single-interest group will often look to multi-interest ones for extending its own membership and legitimacy in communities. It couldn't exist, or at least couldn't be strong, without these broader-based organizations. Thus, it's not realistic to support the single-interest organizations without also supporting the multi-interest ones.

Internal Revenue Service Status

So far we've assumed that the community organizations being looked at are incorporated and have Internal Revenue Service letters indicating they are 501(c)3 organizations. Although those formalities are sometimes questioned on the ground that they are an unnecessary burden for community groups, the advantages of gaining these credentials, on balance, usually outweigh the disadvantages. It's a constructive exercise: meeting the basic requirements for being a not-for-profit corporation, writing bylaws, deciding how the membership is going to be constituted and given authority, and electing a legal board of directors. And if a group wants to raise its own money from foundations, companies, or individuals, it must have the IRS letter. Many donors just have an arbitrary rule that they won't look at a proposal without it.

There certainly can be exceptions, such as when the organization can make a convincing argument for a less formal structure or for depending on a third-party sponsoring agency to receive the grant. But those are circumstances that take special care by both the organization and the funding source, as both sides try to avoid misunderstandings. Contributors have had disappointing experiences with community organizations that were loosely structured for the wrong reasons. Some sponsoring agencies have wanted to keep a community organization in a subordinate, dependent position, "helping it avoid the trouble" of handling its own money, for instance. There have been leaders and staff who have wanted to maintain tighter personal control by discouraging their organizations from becoming incorporated and having a representative board.

The presence of conventional arrangements—such as a board, bylaws, and accounting procedures—makes it more likely that a funder can see what an organization is set up to do and whether it's doing it. Without those arrangements, there had better be some other evidence of organizational clarity and strength. One way or another, the objectives are to get the important facts on the table about legitimacy, competence, focus, and participation and leadership development and to build trust back and forth in effective relationships with good community organizations.

A donor need not wait until the whole credentialing process is completed. Once bylaws are written, the organization has been incorporated, and an application has been filed with the IRS, it is reasonable to consider funding. In the case of a private foundation, if the IRS hasn't yet approved an organization's application for tax-exempt status, the foundation has to assume "expenditure responsibility" for a grant, but that's a straightforward procedure clearly described in IRS regulations. Sometimes helping organizations with early start-up funds in anticipation of their receiving 501(c)3 status is crucial to their development. You can look at the bylaws and the application to the IRS; you can even get a letter from the organization's attorney saying he or she sees no reason why the application shouldn't be handled and approved by the IRS in routine fashion. Compared with the complexities of IRS applications from many other kinds of not-for-profit organizations and agencies, properly written applications from community organizations have raised few questions.

Moving back still further in the evolution of an organization, there are times when a church or a neighborhood center, or an individual with a strong organizing background, wants to start talking with leaders and other residents about pulling together a community organization. As long as it is clear that the support is specifically for this exploratory work, investing in that process can be an important contribution. Depending on how well one knows the people involved, one way of making such a grant something less than just a "license to go fishing" is to insist that, even at this early stage, three or four leaders in the community be aware that a new organization is a possibility so you can talk with them and get their reactions. But the fact that they may show customary skepticism about somebody else's new idea needs to be balanced against your own estimate of the integrity and skills represented by wherever the initiative is coming from.

Your Own Community Agenda

There is no reason why donors shouldn't have their own agenda for community activity. A contributor's perspective will probably include some concerns that are different from those of a community organization—not contrary to the agenda of the community group but complementary to it because they come from a different point of view.

For instance, we've recognized how apprehensive we are about each other in our society. Certainly a common goal of many funding sources is to use their contributions in ways that will improve human relations and understanding in a diverse society—a goal that is especially difficult to achieve under the pluralist constraints of our time. The specifications of chapter 4 and the subsequent descriptions of BUILD, MOP, and UNO show the role that active participation can play in helping us get to know and understand each other through the activities of community organizations.

I especially like Vicki Ceja's remark about how she and other Denver people were now able to see differences *among* their fellow MOP members from Adams County. They were no longer just identifiable as different from Denver city people. That, chances are, is human relations progress. "The circle opens up," she said. Then there was Mary Ellen Montes's similar comment about UNO enlarging the circle, and Gary Rodwell's experience of "a chance to touch the lives" of the members of a white middle-class church, and vice versa.

So to meet the objectives of your own community agenda, you want the community organization you support to contribute to this enhanced exposure and improved relationships among different kinds of communities. That means the membership should become not only good at articulating their own needs and ideas but also good listeners, tolerant of other people's points of view, with an eye to new relationships outside the community. That's probably not a major objective for the organization, especially if it's fairly new. It may not even be on their list of objectives at all during an early time when it's essential for them to establish new strengths within their own community. Reducing prejudices among communities isn't something that is going to happen overnight, in any case. But it's important to you and your goals to have an organization you support eventually take its proper place in constructive social intercourse with other communities and institutions. So you urge the organization to establish connections with outsiders who can be strategically useful in the short run and partners in an inter-community, intercultural process in the longer run. And you encourage those connections whenever you can. Knowing a few of the organization's leaders and knowing some other relevant people, you are in a key "bridge" position to do so.

A related item on philanthropy's agenda is that our funding choices should help us all avoid physical violence in our communities. It's important to try to sort out one's feelings about that in a society where the chance of violence affects how we feel and behave. Philanthropy has traditionally been accused of having a role as a form of social control—keeping the lid on, giving a little help to the poor, and isolating them so they will "behave well," to use M. J. Heale's wry terminology. Grants to community organizations of the kind exemplified in chapter 5 express a conviction that we have replaced that negative tradition with something more fruitful. The security we seek will come not from attempts to control but from efforts to enhance the chances for social and economic participation in American democracy among those who haven't had their share of such opportunities. Funding their own community organizations is an important part of that process.

Another valuable agenda concern for foundations and other sources of philanthropy is helping to keep the community organization's attention on organizing—on the processes of building broader and deeper participation and leadership development in the face of heavy temptations to digress in other directions. This, too, is an especially appropriate role because funding sources and other professional outsiders have long been guilty of encouraging community groups to spend time doing all sorts of other things, such as providing social services or getting deep into the housing or economic development business, which call for very different skills, structures, and loyalties.

Sometimes leaders and staff members of community organizations are tempted in those other directions anyway, because when the organizing work gets hard, service and development activity begins to look attractive, easier, more like a regular 9-to-5 job. But when an organization's leaders and staff start spending time doing these things—thinking in terms of services and development projects and cultivating the dependent relationships with government agencies and others that virtually all these activities require— the organization has lost its position as a community organization. A few people have become private entrepreneurs, managers, and service providers. Given proper disciplines of good organizing, it would have been better to get other, more suitable agencies already in place to do the work, or to set up new agencies at arm's length from the basic continuing energies of the community organization. Donors, knowing the temptations, can help strengthen that discipline from the beginning. Service and development work, especially since the cuts in federal programs, really isn't all that great.

There are other pitfalls, too, which a funding source can help an organization avoid in the interests of good organizing. Does the organization seem to be spreading itself too thin across too many issues or too much territory? Or is it concentrating so much on one issue at the moment that it is in danger of developing tunnel vision, without the broader view of community life that is such a strong asset of community organizations? Is it so understaffed that too little work is being done in the neighborhoods around local concerns? A donor who, in time, chooses to become sensitive to such problems and tactful in talking about them is a useful resource in the field.

There is also the part a donor can play in keeping a community organization as a learning center as well as an action center. Strong leaders and staff tend to become action oriented because the organization thrives on *doing* things. But if it's going to be a place where lots of people learn about effective participation, and if they are going to be inventive about solutions to community problems, the organization has to be deliberately educational and reflective. Whether this is a separate function or part of everyday organizing activity has long been an open question. It seems to make good sense for a community organization to bring its members together regularly to reflect on recent experience and on what that experience suggests for the future, as well as to look at alternative ways of addressing new issues. The best examples I know of firsthand are the habits good community organizations have of leaders and staff evaluating an experience together immediately afterwards, the retreats they periodically conduct, the workshops they hold with consultants from organizing training centers and other experts from fields important to current interests, and the discussion groups they have around specific issues when preparing for annual community conventions. I suspect there are other ways to do it, too.

One of the easiest ways a donor can help encourage the members of a community organization to gain insights from what they have done and to see how those insights bear upon what they want to do is to ask for that quality of thoughtfulness in written and oral reports. I always remember a social science researcher from a foundation staff who said the most important evaluation step for a funding source is not to set up elegant research components but to remember always to ask the basic question, "What have you learned?" That question is helpful to the organization no less than to the contributor.

"What have you learned?" is an introspective question. A friendly contributor might also ask a community organization to consider organizing a broader kind of public reflection. One could propose that we need community-based "town hall" forums to discuss all sorts of topics vital to human survival and well-being—some that are currently among community organization interests, others that are not. Becoming the sponsor of community discussions about anything or everything in the world is a heavy burden to put on a community organization, yet such an organization often seems a more appropriate sponsor than some of the agencies that presume to take that role. And perhaps certain issues that have been out of scope or latent for a community organization may become manifested in such discussions as important issues the members then decide they want to address as a community.

Last but not least, grantmakers have been placing strong emphasis on a broad range of community leadership development initiatives. This was the theme of the 1986 Council on Foundations conference; Pres. James A. Joseph led the discussion of what we mean by leadership, what we expect of it, and where we think it's going to come from. He especially made the point that foundation people and others who support community groups are in a particularly good position to help promote leadership development at the grass roots. "Too often," he said, "we wait for leaders to come riding to our rescue on white chargers—heroes rather than ordinary people with extraordinary commitment." Instead, funding sources can actively encourage some of our most essential leadership from backgrounds in the neighborhoods "where issues take on flesh and blood."

The community groups you deal with think of leaders in terms of how well they can encourage others in their own community to get involved and how effectively they can represent the interests of that community in the world outside. It may be part of your agenda to suggest some other roles for such leaders in other settings where you know their participation would be valuable. There is the danger, of course, that such opportunities may divert attention from local community priorities. But the risk is often well-taken; community leaders who are well disciplined in community organizing can serve with distinction on citywide boards, for instance, without losing their loyalty to their community interests.

And then there is one tactical suggestion. Funding sources are interested in making other kinds of grants in communities, such as to institutions, service agencies, cultural events, and development projects. Community organizations should not be considered the only bridges into the neighborhoods, but they are especially useful because they are run by community people themselves and deal directly with life in the area. Relationships with these organizations give funding sources firsthand intelligence about what the felt needs are in communities and what resources are required to realize progress. One gets a grasp of the relatedness among issues and opportunities in a way that helps develop realistic philanthropic priorities. The impacts of United Way, citywide social service agencies, and other large institutions and programs become clearer when viewed from a community organization's consumer perspective.

The Altruist's Role

The risk in talking this way about all the richness of the community organization experience is that some prospective funders will think it too complicated a field to get into. That's interesting, given that some people in philanthropy stay away from community organizations supposedly because these organizations are too simple, too naive, compared with the grand intellectual challenges of elite agencies dealing with fashionable political topics of the day.

The conviction here is that supporting community organizations takes a different kind of sophistication—a sensitive, modest interest in humanity not always found among people involved in philanthropy. And that brings us back to altruism.

This chapter has been concerned with the criteria one uses in investing in a community's own capacities both for taking charge and developing a decent public life within the community and, at the same time, for encouraging its people to reach out and become helpful, contributing parts of larger communities as well. According to Harvard biologist David Layzer, the two strategies needed for generating stronger traits of altruism among all of us are (1) building constructive interaction within groups individually, and (2) cultivating larger circles, "increasingly comprehensive communities." He is troubled about these inward and outward strategies toward altruism because he sees them as competing, and I'm sure in certain biological contexts they are. But in the dynamics of community organizations supported by intelligent philanthropy, they seem complementary and mutually reinforcing.

What better role for a funding contributor than to advance those basic traits of community we so urgently need in our society?

CHAPTER 9

WINNING EFFECTIVE ROLES FOR PROFESSIONALS IN COMMUNITIES

In the process of encouraging and enabling participation, there is something else contributors can do that gets at a continuing, frustrating problem: the poor relationships, or just the lack of relationships, between community organizations and the professional people who work for service or public interest agencies and institutions.

Professionals who practice in communities have the same constituencies as do the leadership and staffs of community organizations—the residents of those communities. These service practitioners and community organization people share the same working environment; no one else has the same firsthand view of community life that they do. They often have the same concerns and develop the same determination to help people. Other kinds of professionals may not actually work inside communities but are pursuing some of the same issues that community groups are, often with similar goals about what needs to be accomplished.

Such professionals frequently have skills and resources useful in realizing such goals. Yet their contacts with community organizations are usually minimal at best, and their skills and resources seldom get applied to community problems. It's worth looking at how they might be encouraged to play more effective roles.

Advocacy

The issues of the 1960s, 1970s, and 1980s have made many social workers, lawyers, educators, planners, and other professional practitioners feel frustrated with the limitations of their traditional tasks vis-à-vis the needs of poor people. The hardships of poverty and discrimination are more explicit than they used to be, and both professionals and their clients have become more aware of how professional services so often fail to improve the quality of life of poor people. Troubled, embarrassed, sometimes rejected, and increasingly perceptive about the difficulties their clients have, some professionals have looked for ways to help clients by becoming more assertive in representing their clients' rights and interests. This is called advocacy. Advocating for clients—trying to get for them something they deserve to have—has frequently been a radical break with professional convention.

Like all shifts in practice, however, advocacy has produced its own set of professional problems. Heinz Eulau, in a presidential address to the American Political Science Association, expressed a frequent concern when he said, "Paradoxically, its radical appearance notwithstanding, advocacy implies an essentially paternalistic attitude." It is difficult for professional practitioners to avoid that accusation, considering the way advocacy roles are ordinarily played out. When a social worker turns activist and cuts through a lot of red tape to win benefits for a client, it is a great good turn. The client is grateful and the social worker feels useful. Perhaps tragedy has been averted. But often each of the social worker's efforts at advocacy helps only one client once, underscores the helplessness of the client, encourages a dependency relationship between client and professional, and secures more rigidly than ever a bureaucratic system full of doors to which only professional helpers have keys.

When a lawyer contributes his or her services to help a low-income family keep its home, it is the lawyer's position and skill that wins the day. The lawyer's strong authoritative role in such a case is virtually required by the justice system. If a lawyer devises a lawsuit on behalf of a group of poor people who feel they are being discriminated against, he or she may try to involve at least some of the clients in the beginning of the process. But as the case evolves and tangles itself through the months and years, it is the attorney's case to pursue and win or lose. The lawyer is in charge, an advocate whose clients—those who know their attorney at all—appear to have little choice but to accept his or her direction.

The same is true of a planner who fears that some community people are going to be victims of an urban renewal project and decides to do personally whatever is possible to prevail upon administrative offices and legislatures to change the plan, or of an architect who calls for either more or less enforcement of housing code requirements, depending on which change he or she believes will bring more relief to lower-income families. Even with conscientious efforts to counteract the arbitrariness of what they do, such professionals can't escape from the fact that the conventional balances of authority between professional and client are all too often missing when professionals donate time, skill, and influence on behalf of poor people. Lacking both the wherewithal to seek out and pay for the professional services most appropriate to their needs and the status to play an active part in determining the course of advocacy, poor clients tend to have their second-class citizenship emphasized rather than relieved in relationships with professional practitioners who are, it seems, doing them a favor.

Vicki Ceja of MOP shows she knows all about what can go wrong with advocacy when she uses the term to describe a stance that MOP avoids. In talking about a neighborhood victory, she says, "The experience paid off tremendously because neighborhood people led the way and did the work. MOP didn't become some advocacy group doing it for those families."

It is not the intention here to criticize professional pro bono advocacy efforts. On the contrary, these activities and the desires for justice and progress that inspire them can be tremendously valuable. But from our perspective here, perhaps we can see an additional positive dimension of advocacy that can work against the limitations noted by Eulau, helping to increase the benefits that advocacy relationships can bring while reducing the paternalism. The proposition here is that much of the professionals' advocacy should be aimed not at trying to solve their clients' problems for them but rather at strengthening the hand of their clients' community activity, through which clients can work with others in improving their situations themselves. Here are four ways that can be done.

(1) *Advocacy for links between services to individuals and community activities that address the underlying problems.* For instance,

employment services are critically important today. A professional agency offering one-to-one counseling, training, and placement services to unemployed poor people is meeting a need, indeed. Yet it's an expensive program, it can only serve a small percentage of those in need, its capacities for developing a lot of new jobs for clients and others like them are limited, and it can hardly be expected to tackle effectively all the problems within and outside the community that cause the disastrous conditions of unemployment and underemployment. It must become clear to the agency and the community that the agency's program is but one piece and that the major potential for beginning to solve unemployment problems lies first within the initiatives of a strong organization.

In a jobs program of such an organization, community residents, including the clients of the professional agency, can get together to push for job opportunities that may not now be available to people in that community, for training programs of types and capacities far beyond the resources of the present professional agency, and for a community attitude that motivates people in ways the agency could never do on its own. Then, being community people who don't put problems into separate little pigeonholes, they can also understand that if their children are to have a chance at employment in the future, the schools in the community have to be better. And then they can make other connections, identifying the need for community support systems for people who get laid off, for better day care resources, and so on. UNO's work in pressing for the new skills centers of Chicago City Colleges is a good example of this type of activity. So, of course, is BUILD's organizing of the Commonwealth Agreements in Baltimore. The community begins to take charge of solving its problems.

It doesn't happen easily. There aren't a lot of us just plain citizens in any community who are ready to jump at the chance of taking responsibility, whereas there are plenty of us who are willing to assume that professionals are wiser and should be given the responsibility for initiating change. But professional practitioners in the community—instead of encouraging that assumption, which some of them do—can operate from the principle that substantial change isn't going to happen without initiatives from *within* the community. Then they can begin to work with their own clients about becoming active, responsible participants.

(2) *Advocacy for community-based governance of service agencies.* Private agencies providing social work, housing, medical, educational, economic, cultural, or recreational services in communities are not community organizations under our definition here. They are community service or development agencies, discrete services being delivered to the community by a board and staff. But they can work toward one of the key attributes of community organizations by becoming strong institutional assets of the community, run by boards of community people. The benefits are in the community ownership, the accurate matching of programs to needs, the invention of ways in which the agency can help realize the development of other community assets, and the leadership development that comes from those experiences. The agency becomes an enabling institution of the community. No one is in a better position to promote this state of affairs than the professionals involved in such agency programs.

(3) *Advocacy for links between policy and practice.* When professionals, on behalf of their clients, try to win significant change in the way big institutional systems work, it is often easier to get a change in policy than a change in actual practice. Changes can be won in the policies of government housing agencies about code inspections, of school boards about decision making at individual schools, of corporations about hiring and training. But if reform efforts around such matters as these are limited to professional contact with central authorities, there is little assurance that the results will yield improvements on a community level. Changes may be inconsequential or may do more harm than good, and anyway, bureaucracies have a way of absorbing and diminishing change before it gets to the public. Solid, beneficial change seldom occurs when negotiated just among professionals. Only if community people affected by the situation are involved in the process will there be a strong link between the achievement of reform in policy and community insistence that the change produce real improvements for community people. Professional practitioners, with their focus on community clients and their interests in policy as well, can help make that happen.

(4) *Advocacy for including poor people in national deliberations that affect them.* I have commented before on the middle-class nature of national deliberations—by which I mean deliberations about our nation, not something national in the fifty-state sense. If we as a nation are going to consider the changes in basic rules that are being proposed with increasing insistence by, for instance, those who have been calling for a constitutional congress, we need to broaden the deliberating public to include more lower-income people—not just because it's fair but also because they have much of the crucial firsthand experience in many of the issues being raised. Without them at the table we are depending on inadequate information. Insisting on that representation and helping to make it happen effectively needs to be part of a professional discipline. And "effectively" means not settling for token isolated individuals lifted up and out of their communities, but rather pushing for an organizing process that takes the nation's issues to poor communities and generates the type of interest that will yield informed involvement.

Extending advocacy in these ways is a difficult challenge for professional practitioners. Some of the suggestions are not in keeping with what practitioners may feel they need to do to protect and advance their careers. Insisting that the type of direct services professionals provide are only a small part of what needs to happen in a community may seem a stance that threatens to diminish one's professional role. To those who value their position as a professional bridge of advocacy between clients and authorities, any notion of encouraging people to build their own bridges or to fill in the moat can sound like self-destruction. The idea of increasing the community governance of social service agencies, instead of recruiting comfortable, safe outsiders who respect professional authority, can sound personally risky to professionals working for these agencies.

But the alternatives are proving to be even more occupationally hazardous. Those who have supported the 1980s cuts in public funding of social services have justified the move with sweeping conclusions about how such services don't do much good, anyway. And there has been little challenge to that claim. Until those services that are of real value become part of the fabric of communities that need them, closely linked with a lot of other things going on that are judged worthwhile, neither the services nor the professionals involved in them have a constituent voice in the community for the rest of us to hear and respect. Given the current mood of the country to challenge and cut back services, this is risky isolation for professionals.

In contrast, the prospects for professional work within our four examples of advocacy are impressive, indeed. Not the least important factor is the freedom from Eulau's accusation. These advocacy roles work away from paternalism and help communities realize their own potentials.

People engaged in philanthropy who are concerned with what's going to work best for the community are in a strong position to become influential in persuading professional practitioners to extend their understanding of advocacy. Social service agencies that show awareness and skills in working with clients on their community participation should be recognized as having a valuable extra dimension of usefulness well worth supporting.

Consulting

David G. Smith, writing about "Professional Responsibility and Political Participation," takes a conservative, dim view of professional people getting too involved in public affairs. But then he lists the "three legitimate concerns" of a professional with respect to his or her community: "the interests of a reasonably determinate body of clients (or students), the integrity of his profession, and *the expert information needed by the community in reaching decisions* [Emphasis added]."

That last is the gist of consulting. David Easton, delivering another American Political Science Association presidential address, identified teaching and research at one end of an academic professional's potential spectrum of activity, direct involvement in politics at the other, and "somewhere between these," the usefulness of being "a consultant and an advisor."

Consulting to community organizations can be a rewarding professional role for both service practitioners and scholars. Groups tend to listen to, value, and put to good use the information provided by an attorney about housing law, a traffic engineer about one-way streets and stoplights, an economist about local employment trends, a social worker about changes in welfare policies, or a political scientist about how the state legislature works. And such consultants often learn a good deal in return. It can be an unusual opportunity to integrate one's need to serve the community on its own terms and one's need to use and enhance professional skills.

Beyond answering specific questions about the immediate subject at hand, consulting professionals have an opportunity to strengthen the community organization process. While their specific expertise is winning a group's attention, they can promote

- *Attention to a community's own resources and strengths.* The first challenge to any outsider is to help the community become more aware of what it has available within the community to work with. The resources don't leave when the professional goes home.

- *A clearer delineation of issues in the community.* In the previous chapter we saw how people who work for funding sources may have an arm's length view of community affairs that complements a community organization's direct expression of felt needs. The same is true of professional consultants. They can encourage care in determining where the real problems lie, helping people make the connections between immediate tangible concerns and the less visible origins and related conditions of those concerns. They can try to introduce what they feel are important latent questions not yet manifested in the daily life and discourse of the community.

- *A look at alternatives.* Similarly, a professional can encourage community groups to consider a broader range of solutions to problems. Community organizations are at their best when inventive because their approaches come directly out of community experience. Professional consultants can be a stimulating resource to promote that inventiveness by helping a group look at its options. What route do you take in trying to get better education for your children? Better teachers? More money? More supportive parents? Preschool programs? After-school programs? More community control? A new school? Placing the emphasis on alternatives especially helps a consultant avoid the burden of having an organization hear only one plan—for instance, the consultant's own favorite idea of the moment.

- *A holistic approach to problems.* One of the specifications in chapter 4 called for encouraging a holistic perspective on community affairs rather than piecemeal attention to single issues. Even community residents, whom we have credited with having a firsthand full view of life, can become obsessed with single-interest preoccupations. Consultants can turn their distant wide-angle view of the community from a liability into an asset by helping people keep their eyes on as broad a slice of life as possible.

- *Sensible participation by community leaders in the activities of larger arenas.* Community organization leaders get opportunities to be involved in larger circles—boards, committees, advisory positions. As we have said, that's good for everybody—the leader, the community, the larger community, all of us. The challenge to the leader is to do this successfully while still keeping one foot firmly in the community so he or she can retain the ability to understand conditions and to represent the values of that community. That is a difficult task. A professional consultant in the field of interest can help a leader reconcile the conditions and needs of his or her local community with those of a larger arena.

Just as in advocacy, the challenge to the professional consultant is to be useful to the community while avoiding any weakening of community initiative and control. Funding sources can encourage community organizations to include consultants in their plans and budgets and can help them make good connections with prospective candidates. At the same time, when donors consider requests for funding from professional agencies, they can look for evidence of appropriate, effective community consulting activity.

Public Interest Professionals

"Public interest agencies and organizations" seems a fitting name
for the more elite, "downtown" civic initiatives addressing particular problems of corruption, injustice, and ineptness in our society. Those who create and run these agencies and organizations
are therefore public interest professionals. Their emphasis is on
issues and change, not on services to individuals as has been the
case with the professional practitioners. Some agencies and organizations define themselves in terms of their *constituencies*—women,
senior citizens, blacks, Hispanics, gays, immigrants, and parents.
Others define themselves in terms of their chosen *interests* that are
not so constituency-specific: civil liberties, the environment, energy
costs, economic development, good government, affordable housing, open housing, urban planning, peace, voter registration, population, public interest law, and effective law enforcement.

Most groups represent convictions that have become articulated
in just the past twenty-five years. Most would be called liberal or
progressive in their politics though there are significant exceptions,
both those that span a broad ideologically conservative spectrum
and those that have become the conservative voices in specific areas
of interest: "right to life" agencies, the network of conservative
public interest law agencies, and national conservative research and
planning institutes, for instance.

Staffing and governance of these initiatives are predominantly
middle class, regardless of their political inclinations. So are most
of the active constituents, even when it seems logical that they
should include poor people. The style is professional; those in
charge have status in the fields of interest, often including academic
credentials. They do a lot of networking and do most of their work
on an entrepreneurial level with their professional peers. These
agencies and organizations are, after all, part of pluralist arrangements, and their structure and activities show the influences of that
design.

I favor a distinction between organizations and agencies because
it leads to better understanding. Public interest *organizations* organize substantial numbers of people. The people who identify with
the organization are usually called members; they become impor-

tant in giving the organization a sense of public identity in political action, in fund raising, and in developing leadership for the organization. Public interest *agencies*, on the other hand, rely on a much more compact setting: the staff and board along with a relatively small circle of loyal supporters. Those involved in such agencies feel confident about what they are doing and insist that the legitimacy of their work will be measured in terms of its consequences rather than who belongs.

In looking at these two pairs of distinctions, we might assume organizations to be constituency-oriented and agencies to be interest-oriented, but that's not always the case. An organization may be a women's group (constituency-oriented) or a similarly large membership-based group concerned, perhaps, about the environment (interest-oriented).

One other clarification is helpful in thinking about these organizations and agencies vis-à-vis efforts to promote participation. They may do a lot of organizing, but it's organizing "from-the-top-down" rather than a process that invests community people with the responsibility and opportunity for making basic decisions and developing programs. For instance, a public interest agency or organization may reach out and ask community organizations to come get involved in its work, but the agenda is set and activities are led by professionals and civic leaders who do not belong to the communities in question, particularly poor communities.

It might seem logical to expect that links between community organizations and these public interest agencies and organizations would be strong. Since there are often shared convictions and common goals for the community, it would seem natural to work together for mutual benefit. A community organization in a poor community can gain technical knowledge and contacts from a planning agency or a public interest law firm or a senior citizens organization. Members can learn about different approaches to problems. In return, the community organization's participation can sharpen the public interest group's understanding of needs and issues, give authentic consumer critiques of strategic options and help invent some more, and provide grass-roots energy for change to complement the activities of the public interest group.

But in our experiences trying to fund those combinations, several of us have learned that it isn't as easy as it sounds. Too many community organization leaders and staff don't trust the "downtown" public interest people. Too many public interest staff and board members don't believe they need to validate their positions by investing so much of their precious resources in relationships with community groups. I always remember the moment of truth, or at least candor, when a distinguished environmentalist told me the environmental movement "didn't have time to organize the poor." He said he realized how environmental problems often affected lower-income people more than others (such as the UNO territory becoming a toxic waste dump), but because he had so little contact with them and their communities, he wrote them off and lost the potential strength of their participation.

There are workers on both sides who can tell countless stories of times when they have tried to build bridges between public interest professionals and community organizations. But phone calls weren't returned, the timing was wrong, or people ultimately just didn't quite understand each other. It seems eventually to come down to being a cultural problem, with different perspectives and habits. It's just difficult for people from both professional public interest agencies and low-income community organizations to work together in the intense way that each of their complicated, fragile operations require, no matter how sympathetic their values and visions may be to one another.

Once one has recognized the fact that it's not easy, however, there is still every reason to encourage some arrangements that can improve the chances for these precious relationships to work. In the few places and circumstances where that task has been addressed coherently, we have barely begun to identify what it takes. But we know some of the necessary ingredients: (1) people assigned to the task on both sides who are more sensitive and patient than most, (2) an understanding that the strength of the collaboration lies as much in the differences of style as in the similarities of convictions, (3) agreement on realistic objectives for collaboration to be reached in modest steps, (4) a joint memorandum spelling out who's responsible for what, and (5) set times for frequent reports and meetings.

If a funding source is involved with both public interest agencies and community organizations, it is in a key position to see that this sort of deliberate preparation is carried out. The philanthropist's clear view of both kinds of grantees is especially helpful in encouraging them to be explicit about what their objectives are in getting together and how those objectives fit in with other goals and organizational needs on each side.

Community organizations and public interest agencies and organizations do need each other, though not necessarily equally. To cite the example of public schools again, we have had years of intense professional attention to the problems of the nation's big-city school systems, and those systems are generally working worse than before. It is increasingly evident that no effective progress will be made until there is significant improvement in the extent and intensity of community participation—parents, students, and other community people becoming involved in making the schooling experience a much more successful one. The initiatives described in chapter 5 show how community organizations are the key to developing that involvement. Public interest agencies seeking improvements in schools and other aspects of community life need to establish working relationships with community organizations—not just to be nice but to win.

Three types of public interest agencies and organizations need special note because they often seem to become confused with community organizations themselves:

(1) *Voter registration programs.* There has been great renewed interest in voter registration activity among funding sources and others seeking new ways to help empower poor people. Several new agencies have been established in the 1980s, working nationally or regionally to comply with the IRS stipulation that foundations can make specified grants for voter registration only to those programs that operate in five states or more. These agencies often use community organizations either as local representatives in building a registration program or just as a way of gaining access into communities.

Many enthusiasts about voter registration appear to believe that a good voter registration drive is really all that it takes to lift a community out of powerlessness and establish its people as true participants in the American system. That's too bad. Voting is great for electing people. But holding them accountable, telling them what to do, and giving them the constituent pressures they need to be effective in government is a different kind of community work. Key to *that* activity is the independent community organization, without whose persistent on-site effort the elected official drifts away under the pressures of other interests, and disappointment and disillusionment about the value of voting again prevail among the poor. To enhance participation in any meaningful way, it doesn't make sense to support the limited activities of voter registration drives without giving more substantial and consistent support to the broader field of community organizing.

Voter registration drives and community organizations do share one constructive feature: their emphasis on local affairs. Right now seems a time when the only political figure most Americans relate to closely is the president. He is our popular national representative; we vote him into office and then he keeps in touch with us through the media. But that is hardly a satisfactory way to have political representation, so it is important to encourage arrangements that bring some of that political attention back home, where we are more distinguishable parts of smaller electorates and can have more realistic connections with politicians. Both voter registration drives and community organizations help do that by promoting continuing participation in these more intimate political circumstances. Community organizations with 501(c)3 status don't elect representatives or support candidates, but they establish the kind of relationships that can make the representatives better politicians and us better voters and constituents.

(2) *Large "umbrella" organizations.* Some people who are eager to press for social change, including former organizers of community groups, have become convinced that solutions to our problems will emerge only through work on national, regional, and state levels. They have organized around issues at those levels, bringing in whatever community organizations can be attracted. Their lists of participating community organizations, and the presence of selected leaders from some of the organizations, give these umbrella groups their validity in approaching public and private forces in Washington, state capitols, and national corporate board rooms. This type of activity has been especially appealing to those funding sources that have decided they want to be involved in national movements.

It is certainly true that community organizations need to get together and address some of their needs jointly in larger arenas. The hazard is that the umbrella organizations tend to be created by strong entrepreneurial personalities, who develop their own national or regional agenda and then organize from the top down. They have taken issues away from community organizations, and they have attracted leaders out of communities into new, exotic, and usually temporary roles in a manner that doesn't encourage the leaders to keep one foot firmly planted back on home turf. The organizers have made connections in high places with public and private executives who appreciate their sophistication. Positions are being taken and negotiations carried out supposedly in the name of community people, but without much substance of representation and involvement.

The only solution to that problem is to have enough bona fide community organizations around the country strong enough to insist that they be part of national processes, through either existing umbrella arrangements or new ones that are actually governed by the community organizations themselves.

(3) *Management assistance agencies for community groups.* Another type of applicant popular among funding sources has been the agency that proposes to give management assistance to community organizations and community-based agencies. Again, there is no doubt that such help is needed; the list of what a contributor is supposed to look for in evaluating a community organization (chap. 8) suggests how difficult it is to run one of these organizations effectively. Leaders and staff need help. But an odd phenomenon can be seen in the annual reports of some foundations. They show grants to an impressive array of agencies dedicated to giving community groups every conceivable type of management assistance—legal, accounting, board and staff training, strategizing, networking, fund raising, public relations, art, whatever. The same grants lists, however, show little if any support for the community groups themselves, the ones that presumably need these services.

That's a suspicious situation. People of various professional backgrounds who want to help community agencies and organizations have access to funding sources, can be very convincing about how the people of poor communities need their services, and are able to write good proposals for the funding of their management assistance programs. The proposals are appealing to funders. Instead of having to cope with innumerable applications from all sorts of grass-roots organizations and agencies and make judgments about them, here is a very articulate plan from someone who promises to help these community groups. This is trickle-down philanthropy, supporting agencies that are not part of poor communities and looking forward to the good that such support may ultimately do for the less fortunate, without also supporting the organizations in those communities directly.

What especially hurts in the popularity of these three types of public interest agencies is that the foundations and other funding sources that have been so enthusiastic about voter registration programs, that have been so attracted to national "coalitions" and other umbrella agencies, and that have chosen to make grants to management assistance agencies rather than to community groups themselves are the very sources one would hope would be in the front ranks of those interested in supporting participation itself. They obviously appreciate how philanthropy can play a role in public affairs, and they show concern about the troubles of poor people in this country. But they have decided not to make grants to community organizations, where people are most likely to get their essential participation experience.

Professionals in Philanthropy

Thus the discussion of professional people and their relationships with communities comes around to the subject of professionals in philanthropy. There is some question about the applicability of the title *professional* to such staff people; they have not been academically trained specifically for careers in giving away money. But in a broader definition, the term is used commonly for people who do the program work of philanthropy.

Foundation and other funding source staff people are subject to the same habits general to the field of philanthropy (see chap. 6). They tend to want to give to peers instead of to the poor, to support major institutions and the professions, and to be partial to the medical model of philanthropy. Their status as employees compounds these inclinations. It is ordinarily safer for staff people in philanthropy to recommend that funds go to organizations run by either their own peers or peers of those who employ them, or both. The relationship between donor and donee then seems more likely to be based securely on clear agreements and expectations among like-minded people. If the funded activity fails to measure up to expectations, it is easier for the donor and the donee to forgive each other and it may also be easier to learn something from the experience. For much the same reasons, it makes sense for professionals in most philanthropic settings to prefer contributions to major institutions and agencies, those that are professionally run. And the medical model is appealing in the way it produces narrowly defined proposals that are easy to interpret to board members and others, and that are about interesting specific projects with clear predictions of obviously worthwhile consequences.

At the same time, professionals in philanthropy are generally attracted, as are other professionals, to those relationships that will improve the quality of their own lives on the job and enhance their careers. Such self-interests also lead them to favor working relationships with peers or, better, people with whom they would like to be peers. There are practical values in becoming unusually knowledgeable about those specific fields of beneficiaries that are most likely to yield future career opportunities. And with a desire for professional progress, there is a natural bias in favor of those philanthropic experiences in which one copes successfully over time with tasks of increasing complexity.

Supporting community organizations doesn't easily match these inclinations of a philanthropic staff. Community organizing has not yet become a professional field itself, nor is there yet much of an accessible, organized body of knowledge. The work is done by volunteer community leaders and notoriously underpaid staff members; neither are considered peers or role models by most professionals in philanthropy. Further, many of the day-to-day issues involved in the work of organizing in a poor community are not the same as those that have the best occupational and social currency elsewhere in the world. The first community organization action to improve garbage pickups is okay, but experiences repeated on that level become less exciting as time goes on. Of course, garbage collection is not the ultimate goal of the community organization's program. Community people at work to realize the American dream have to address this and all sorts of other issues to get there. But the immediate topic's lack of appeal to the philanthropic professional becomes a community organization's disadvantage in raising money.

Even the "larger," more potentially attractive issues community organizations attend to can be relatively uninteresting to professional grantmakers, just in the way community groups go about the task. When one is surrounded by various professionals and academics who have sophisticated theories about how things ought to be in urban schooling, energy policies, industrial development, and welfare reform, investing in the pragmatic processes of even a BUILD, MOP, or UNO can be frustrating. That's particularly the case in the beginning. MOP's careful approach to the job of getting parents involved in school affairs is starting with months and months of attention to the threshold questions and winnable issues that parents identify. Only later will they begin to talk about some fascinating new grand designs.

So there are good reasons why one doesn't find community organizations from poor communities high up on the grants lists of many funding sources. Many professionals who might be interested find their progressive satisfactions elsewhere by giving to a more professional, middle-class array of public interest agencies and organizations.

How to overcome these obstacles to reach a broader acceptance of community organizations as an object for philanthropy is a difficult question. I offer two hunches about strategic directions. First, much of any new interest in the support of citizen participation through community organizations is likely to come from the laypeople who govern philanthropic resources, rather than from staff or professional advisers. Board or committee members of funding sources don't have to be as encumbered with mixed motives as the employed philanthropic practitioners are. Thus, they can better afford to take the first step in offering the longer, broader community view. Perhaps they are more the altruists.

Second, for the longer run, we need to look to our occupation of philanthropy and nudge it along toward its own maturity as a career that has some shared principles, experiences, and analysis among its practitioners. So many of the best and brightest grant-makers shouldn't have to feel that they must soon reach outside of philanthropy itself for their careers and attach themselves to other fields that command the respect and rewards lacking for all but a few in philanthropy. They should be able to feel that philanthropy itself allows them to pursue objectives that they and their colleagues and board members have carefully developed and articulated, in the context of an increasingly mature sense of what philanthropy is for and how it works. At that point, a program to enhance democratic participation by funding community organizations becomes an impressive professional philanthropic opportunity. We will have, then, a growing number of practitioners in the field of philanthropy who understand what community organizations are doing and want them to keep on doing it and doing it better.

All foundations and other funding resources aren't going to want to reach for such a level of reflection and purposefulness, but it would be great if we could increase the percentage who do.

Research

There are important opportunities in community-based research on several levels. Some involve what is essentially fact finding to help inform the strategies of various agencies and community organizations themselves. When a community group gets involved in activities about unemployment, for instance, some research is needed to answer basic questions about what the job preferences and skills are among unemployed and underemployed people in the community and where the opportunities are that match them. Professionals trained in this type of investigating can help a community group organize the questions and the research. When properly advised, members of the community group will make good researchers. One way to help ensure that the findings will be used is to have the research process become a community enterprise.

Then there is research on the impact of big centralized public systems. We talk all the time about welfare, schools, and the courts, yet we seldom have solid independent information about how those systems affect people in a community setting. One way for professionals in research to frame the right questions, get to the right people for answers, and then see that the results of the research are understood and applied to the task of reforming these systems is to work closely with community organizations.

And there is research of a less pragmatic kind, particularly about human behavior. So much of the recent behavioral research referred to earlier has suffered from assumptions about community people, especially poor people, that were distant and wrong. For instance, with respect to one of the expectations identified in chapter 1, numerous researchers have created unreal distinctions between private and public interests. Poor people, it is said, can't be interested in becoming publicly active because they are too preoccupied with meeting basic private needs for survival. That is an understandable middle-class assumption. Public activity in the more affluent circles of our society is regarded as a charitable, civic contribution, something you do in your spare time, having nothing to do with the private paid work you do for food and shelter. People in poor communities, on the other hand, find no such division. They know they have to get together in a common public life to try to win a decent level of these private necessities. That link between private and public is the first appeal community organizations in such communities have among their members. As noted before, it is the prime answer to gloomy predictions of noninvolvement, with far more relevance and urgency in it than a social scientist's assumption of public life as something apart.

Misconceptions such as this skew research designs. When research is based on such errors, the questions are wrong, the findings are wrong, and the judgments based on the findings are wrong. Scholars were persuaded to become more careful in poor communities in the '60s and '70s, so there is now perhaps more awareness of such hazards than there used to be. Political scientist David Easton urges the profession to question its prejudices and values so that unexamined premises won't "determine the selection of problems and their ultimate interpretations." Close relationships with community organizations can contribute a great deal to cultivating that attention. Although most private funding sources haven't customarily been asked for support for research, that may be changing because of cuts in public funding. When private grantmakers are asked to fund research, they can perform a service that public sources have seldom performed, seeing to it that links are established early in the planning stages between the research project and community groups.

Something becomes especially clear after we have rambled through several of these relationships between poor communities and professional outsiders. Such relationships, when negative, can become so pervasive that they define the community. John McKnight calls these "client communities," in which people are not producers or even effective consumers, but rather dependent clients of service systems.

McKnight, who is director of community studies at Northwestern University's Center for Urban Affairs and Policy Research, has worked harder than anyone else I know to get down to some truths about our American systems and make them coherent. His conclusion about services and the helping professions is a challenge to community organizations, funding sources, and the service professionals themselves:

> I recognize that it is difficult for people of good will to believe that human service systems and helping professions could be damaging to those they seek to assist. Nonetheless, after thirty years of neighborhood work, it is my conclusion that the profound difference about a client neighborhood is that its people are walled in by the systems and professions that speak for them, have authority over them, and interpret them to the public.
>
> The first step toward building bridges outward is to break through that wall. Inventive independent philanthropy could collaborate with regenerating neighbors and neighborhoods in legitimizing local voices and magnifying images of capacity.

That statement testifies to the importance of community organizations, but it also can help guide a philanthropist's progress in his or her relationships with professionals who use community settings as their workplace, encouraging them to win more effective roles in serving those communities constructively.

CHAPTER 10

TRACING THE INITIAL EXPERIENCE: OPTIONS AND OPPORTUNITIES IN FUNDING

If you are new to this field of community organizations, visit one or two to see what they are doing and who is involved in the leadership and staff. Begin comparing what you see with the evaluation criteria of chapter 8. The ease of finding organizations will depend on the community characteristics within whatever urban or rural territories are appropriate for you.

Other people can suggest what organizations to see and go with you on a field visit, if you wish. These may be people from foundations, company contributions or community relations departments, churches and church denomination offices, regional associations of grantmakers (see app. II), occasionally the social science departments of colleges and universities, other local agencies and organizations you know and respect, training centers specifically in this field (see app. I), areawide management assistance agencies, or umbrella agencies (see chap. 9).

Remember that you have to be very clear in describing what you're looking for because of the misconceptions people have. You are not looking for social service agencies or housing or economic development agencies. Instead, you are looking for broad-based organizations of community people in poor communities who are addressing issues they hold in common in ways that will benefit significant numbers of people in the community. The issues may be about jobs, schools, housing, crime, city services, welfare, health, utilities—whatever community needs people are trying to meet, partly by their own invention, partly by winning changes in how they are served by outside institutions and agencies.

Referrals from others should be sought, based not so much on other people's favorite organizations but rather on just the organizations they know to be strong or potentially strong. Even so, the suggestions you get will be selective; a variety of information sources is advisable.

Make an appointment and meet volunteer leaders as well as staff. The most important things to look for on a first visit are (1) what kind of people are active in the organization, and (2) what sort of work they're doing or want to do. This information begins to give you what you need to apply the evaluation criteria, even just tentatively.

As you're doing that, you begin to identify what seems important to those active in the organization and how that gibes with your own sense of values and those of others involved philanthropically with you. Do you respect the organization's priorities and how it proposes to pursue them? If you have questions, can you ask them and get satisfactory answers that give you some new insights? Do you begin to see some ways in which support for such an organization would truly help a substantial number of people work on problems?

A procedural question at this stage is what do you need that you don't already have to do a good job of supporting such organizations? Perhaps nothing at the moment. But early experience may show the need for a suitable full- or part-time staff person who would be comfortable and effective in working with you in this field, for an expansion of your board to include people especially interested in this field, for closer links to other sources of funding, or for a statement of purpose that includes the support of community organizations. Before selecting staff or board members, be sure you and they have a common understanding of what a community organization is and what it does.

Your chances of finding one or two community organizations nearby that have a track record and can be evaluated as going concerns are maybe fifty-fifty. At any given time, most of our largest cities have examples. There are also groups in some smaller urban areas, some rural groups, and some county and state organizations. It's a question of getting to know the territory and evaluating the condition of the organizing art in whatever area you identify with philanthropically.

If you do find a couple of organizations that seem well worth supporting, at least with modest initial grants through which you can get to know one another, you have a fine opportunity to begin seeing what happens in this field and what characteristics *you* believe are fundamentally important. There is special satisfaction in funding community organizations because you can soon sense the effects of the organizing process as people get together and address community needs.

If your inquiries don't produce established organizations that are up and running and attractive to you, you may settle for some that are in rudimentary beginning stages (as described in chap. 8). The roots of BUILD, MOP, and UNO were modest indeed. Finding embryonic community organizations can be fortunate because such beginnings bring fresh energies to community life. They may include a gathering of a few people around a church or two, or a neighborhood center, or a couple of block clubs, developing their own strength and some notions of joining with others. They may be a group of parents with children at a particular school, or a tenants organization, or an ad hoc group making itself heard on a local issue of the moment—an urban renewal project, plans for a new highway, or something else that is going to affect their neighborhood. Or they may be getting together to win better public services in a particular area of immediate interest—job training and employment opportunities, public aid, medical services, police patrols, housing services, street repairs, or recreation facilities. People in poor communities, just like people in every other kind of community, usually take their first steps as citizens in public life when confronted with specific, tangible issues that affect their lives.

What you are *not* necessarily looking for are the high-visibility, high-profile individuals who may be very useful citizens but have developed such habits of working alone as personalities with just their own coteries that they would very likely have difficulty becoming leaders of real community organizations. As the descriptions of BUILD, MOP, and UNO emphasized repeatedly (chap. 5), leaders of community organizations constantly have to encourage the self-determination and leadership potentials of everyone else in the community. That can be hard for people who have been in the spotlight on their own. Potential community organization leaders are likely to be people you find through other contacts you have in communities—individuals who are respected by other residents for their capacities to listen, work with others, and learn from their experiences, and who won't get too excited about their roles as celebrities the first time they get on television.

You are also looking for organizers, either now at work with good organizations or looking, as you are, for opportunities. They should have some experience and share convictions with you about the principles described in the evaluation criteria. If they are in especially short supply—and good organizers always are—you might contact one or more of the experienced organizing training programs listed in appendix I for suggestions if not specific referrals.

Given some initial opportunities to fund community groups, the experience should begin to be a rewarding one. You will have become an important resource for promoting citizen participation in your communities. While that may be leadership enough for you, as time goes on and you learn something about the universe of community activity in your area, you may also become intrigued with what it would take to encourage a substantial advancement in the field. What needs to be done to cultivate an environment that will convince more existing and potential community leaders, and more potential staff people of high quality, to choose to devote time and talent to community organization activity?

The answer to that question will depend on the characteristics of your communities and on your own insights as you become more familiar with organizing. Certainly none of us claim to have any pat solutions; you will be joining a group of searchers. My own beginning of an answer is that a better local environment for community organizing needs four new ingredients—new, at least, to most places I have visited: (1) conventional management assistance services that extend more effectively to community organizations, (2) more connections among community organizations and between them and outside allies, (3) high-quality training programs for both volunteer leadership and staff, and (4) new ways to attract, recruit, place, and promote community organization staff. All four of these needs lend themselves to some exploration by grantmakers.

(1) *Management assistance.* The first prescription should be the easiest need to fill, one way or another. Many cities and regions have agencies that provide legal, accounting, fund raising, and other administrative assistance to not-for-profit organizations. These are the management assistance agencies discussed earlier. Up to now,

most of them have tended to assist social service, cultural, and economic development agencies more than community organizations. But the same basic administrative skills apply. Whether some existing agencies can help community organizations or a separate resource is called for is a question for local analysis.

(2) *Connections with other community organizations and public interest groups.* The second necessary development calls for some appropriate good office to start bringing community organizations together with each other and with public interest organizations and agencies. Contact with other community groups can be invigorating. Gary Rodwell's comment in chapter 5—"I get to know that we aren't just isolated here"—obviously applies both to relationships within a city or region and to contacts in other parts of the country. And it's practical as well as therapeutic; community organizations can't build trusting coalitions among themselves until they know each other. Somebody has to be deliberately making the introductions.

The other type of connection is the one recognized in chapter 9 as valuable though difficult—working relationships with public interest agencies and organizations. Community organizations and "downtown agencies" that have some commonality of purposes need each other. It's not far-fetched to say that our democracy's problems won't be solved unless and until they get together. But the process requires a lot of nudging and bridging. An agency taking on the responsibility of doing some of the nudging and bridging might also facilitate the advocacy and consultation relationships described in chapter 9. That's a tough assignment calling for patience and diplomacy, but it can serve a tremendous need. Professionals have to be encouraged and counseled, and there is much that community organizations can learn about how to take advantage of technical assistance from professionals. A good book entitled *Doing Good* says succinctly that the challenge for community groups in these relationships is to learn how to "protect themselves against abuse without depriving themselves of the benefits that experts can deliver."

(3) *Training.* The criteria of chapter 8 listed effective training for both leaders and staff as essential to competence in this field. Training has to be integrated into the daily activities of community

organizations. Universities and outside unaffiliated training schools can be useful resources for part of the program, but only for a part. Both on-the-job and long-term in-service training are essential.

It is no coincidence that all three strong community organizations described earlier have close continuing ties to well-respected training resources that work with the groups in their own community settings. Training programs such as these serve not just newly recruited staff and leaders, but whole community organizations in close contractual relationships. Staff directors and experienced lead organizers use the programs to refresh their own skills, to gain mutual support among themselves, and to improve their own capabilities as trainers. Leaders of community groups—the volunteers—come for training and get follow-up support in their own communities. Since training resources serve more than one community organization at a time, their workshops and other activities encourage the interrelationships among groups mentioned above.

Someone in an area, or preferably a diverse group of people interested in improving what's available for the area's communities, needs to take inventory of what training resources are close by, what might be imported effectively from further away, and what qualified advisers might be able to help guide the development of new local resources for training in this community organization field.

(4) *Recruiting staff.* There were times in the 1960s and 1970s when students, members of the clergy, and other volunteers or virtual volunteers filled the ranks of community organization staffs. They were looking for jobs in which they could work for justice and equality and better human relations, and they were willing to work for very little money. Many only worked part time, most only devoted a year or so to the job. There aren't many workers like that today, and it is questionable whether community organizing could ever return to such staffing patterns. Most of those organizers were white. Community groups today need more minority staffing appropriate to most of the communities they serve. They also need longer-term staffing, producing at least a core of more seasoned, well-trained people. And they must be able to talk about career opportunities for well-qualified, ambitious people, includ-

ing decent pay, benefits, and advancement—advancement in terms of both organizing itself and moving on to other logical fields where a background in community organizing is a proven asset.

Community organizing is a hard job that demands an unusual combination of attributes. An organizer needs to be *sensitive*—a good listener who respects constituents; *aggressive* in helping people get together and in facilitating their research, planning, and actions; *analytical* in approaches to problems; *creative and flexible* in encouraging new solutions; *willing to stay in the background* and let leaders lead; *observant* about leadership potentials in others and *knowledgeable* about how to cultivate them; *articulate* in talking with community people and outsiders; *respectful of the attention to detail* required in good organizing; *consistent* in helping to keep the organization on track; *idealistic* enough to keep an eye on longer-range organizational goals while coping with each day's business; and *impressive as a professional* who can gain the respect and trust of strong community leaders.

The best organizers in the United States have all of this or know how they can make up for something that's lacking. They marshal their abilities with a discipline that makes them complete professionals in the best sense of being in charge of what they need to be and do, so that they can work effectively and responsibly in a complex occupation.

Not surprisingly, there aren't very many of them. A lot of men and women who appear to come close to the characteristics just listed are being sought by private industry and government in extensive recruiting programs that are highly competitive. This has, of course, been particularly true of minority candidates. Those of us interested in having some promising candidates pursue careers in community organizing have done virtually nothing to try to compete. The field is relatively unknown, and most pay scales and benefits are absurd compared with what the requirements are. All of that must change if we want good candidates.

Some of the best recruits become identified in the organizing process itself—community people from many different backgrounds who just show natural abilities and inclinations to work effectively, not as leaders but as organizers in their own communities. Then there are prospects who have held jobs in which they have been close to community organizations, such as in community-based agencies, research work, or union experience. And it would be good for influencing future career choices as well as present recruiting if we paid more attention to potential candidates on college and university campuses. A well-placed collaborative effort among community organizations, counselors, faculty members, and perhaps other interested agencies could at least ensure that compelling information about community careers such as organizing is always available on campus.

A deliberate campaign to recruit good candidates for organizing from communities, related fields, campuses, and other sources in a particular area would pick up on a lot of ideas that have proven successful in other occupational categories. For instance, it would develop internship programs, conduct research about careers in community organizing and where they can lead to, and work with community groups and funding sources on improving pay, benefits, and personnel policies. It would also show everyone the creative challenges and valuable experiences of the organizer's job. Moreover, it would become the focal point for all kinds of activities designed to get and keep attention on career potentials in this field and give people a framework within which to become interested and step forward and identify themselves.

One way or another, the recruiting activity has to be closely linked to real job opportunities. At best there should be jobs open, or at least the promise of realistic opportunities in the not-too-distant future.

Much needs to be done in developing local or regional capacities for all four of these components—management assistance, connections among organizations, training for leaders and staff, recruiting staff. Funding sources can play an important role in helping to determine the needs and who can meet them, perhaps in being a good convenor, and in providing part of the funds required to make things possible. In the parts of the country I'm familiar with, that's an intriguing, wide-open opportunity for people in philanthropy who can approach such a situation with sensitivity and patience.

I want to end this chapter with some comments that are in a different category from the rest of this book. Up to now the discussion has been fairly all-inclusive regarding community organizations.

I haven't passed judgment much; who's to say where and how a truly useful community organization may be born and then nourished with the help of private philanthropy? But now some judgments are called for, based on my own experience and on where I think we're going in this field.

Chicago, where I've worked, is called the birthplace of community organizing. At least on a rudimentary level, organizing has become a relatively commonplace activity in Chicago compared with most other places. Certainly some organizations have been useful, both to their own communities and to Chicago as a whole. They have at various times promoted participation, generated leadership, kept important stable families living in communities, solved problems, and improved conditions.

Other community organizations in Chicago, however, have been less useful. I know from personal experience that this city's foundations and corporations have funded and refunded many community organizations that really haven't gone anywhere. Such organizations have reached a minimum level of having an office, a staff person, and a very modest routine of work in the community, and then they have pretty much become static. Sometimes that may be what the leader or leaders wanted—just a little organization to call their own. Other times—more often than not—organizations sincerely try to start developing themselves into strong resources for their communities, but conflicts and disappointments come along and put a cap on the process. Or there is a time of rapid growth and activity that reaches some peak and then rapidly loses strength and settles down at a mediocre level to rest on laurels and relive old victories. In any case, the groups seldom die; they just sit there, taking up space.

For some funding sources in Chicago and elsewhere, such limitations are just fine. They like to show they support grass-roots organizations and are close to the people, but they actually have a low threshold of tolerance for any strong, assertive behavior from the communities or even for signs that more than a handful of people are getting together in an organization. They may say they like the idea of self-help; they may even criticize community groups for not being bigger and more important. But if the organizations do get bigger and more important, such contributors get uncomfortable. A little experience and careful selection shows them that with many groups they can have their cake and eat it, too—plenty of credit for contributing to communities, with virtually no risk of embarrassment or of significant numbers of people getting organized. There may be strong language in their guidelines about supporting communities and organizations run by community people, but what such contributors are really saying with their choices is that they only fund relatively helpless community organizations. It's like an older and much more frequently discussed phenomenon: people who fund or manage social work services in such a way that they help keep clients in poverty rather than deliberately helping them get out of it.

The rest of us in philanthropy may not share this view about promoting only limited participation. We may understand clearly that the concerns on which such inhibitions are based are unfounded and that we all have much more to fear from *not* encouraging effective participation. But we too have been a part of the problem, nonetheless. We have tended to have low standards for community organizations; we have helped a lot of ineffective ones get going and, worse, we have helped them perpetuate themselves. It's been hard to turn down proposals from community groups, especially when we listen to their optimism about how their fresh or refreshed energies are going to change their world. It's easy to let their enthusiasms spring our own hopes once again, so that we tolerate a great many exceptions from our evaluation criteria. But ultimately, the performance of weak community organizations gets discouraging. Then we risk losing those in philanthropy who have championed the support of participation and leadership development. That's a tragedy. It seems worth trying to identify the reasons community organizations congeal and then figuring out how donors might help prevent that from happening.

Five basic reasons seem to say why many—certainly not all—community organizations flatten out and lose their vigor. First, the leaders themselves can limit an organization's constituency, one way or another. Maybe they do it deliberately, or maybe they fail to sell themselves to others. Instead of it becoming an open process with new people, new chunks of neighborhood, new life coming in all the time and producing a flow of workers and leaders, the organization becomes a cadre of a few individuals. Instead of beginning to reach out to other communities and working with other organizations on common objectives, the group builds a wall around its territory and hunkers down inside.

Second, some organizations are just basically too disorganized to grow beyond a certain level. Money isn't handled right. People aren't held responsible for what they say they'll do. There's not enough focus and continuity of effort to make much of anything work.

Third, there's too little vision being applied. Leaders are wise to start out with modest objectives. But they can get locked into activities that after awhile are not just modest but trivial, with few connections to the rich resources of values and hopes and potentials in the community. Once upon a time, when an organization showed such limitations, some of us were in the habit of saying that the organization kept working on only the "chocolate milk issues" of the community, remembering a parents group that had begun and ended its organizing activity with just the question of what was available for their schoolchildren to drink at lunch.

Fourth, right next to vision is a sense of humor, an ability to celebrate whatever good things happen and survive the disappointments and tragedies. In community work in poor communities, that's essential if you're going to stay with it for awhile, yet it's hard for a lot of good, dedicated people to do. There may be humor in the streets and homes, but for the leader or organizer who feels expected to bring some change and improvements to the community, the day-to-day litany of roadblocks and resistances makes it hard to find relief. There are ways to try to ease the habitual grimness; a community organization's social life needs to be just as inventive as the organization's plans for cutting down on lead and asbestos poisoning. But sometimes that agenda item doesn't get much priority. Then the community's image of the organization becomes unattractive, and leadership becomes less effective.

And fifth, when there is some success, it can bring internal, interpersonal problems that are too tough for an organization to cope with. Even with the best of initial training and admonitions, it's hard for leaders to anticipate what pressures are going to build up when their organization gets to a point where some of the leaders, some of the neighborhoods, get chances to reach for advantages not open to the rest of the organization.

Gary Rodwell of Baltimore's BUILD speaks of the "many times

we've reached crises and would have fallen into traps—vested interests of some members against others, turf wars." At Denver's
MOP, leaders and staff recognize the dangers when a few reach
a level of "super-empowerment." When those internal crises come,
a community organization may fall apart, it may survive and move
ahead, or it may retreat to a less ambitious level of activity where
the pressures aren't so heavy. The last of these three scenarios happens a lot. It's especially painful because the troubles involved,
by definition, were a clear sign that the organization was beginning to reach its potential.

How can a community organization have the best chance to overcome these five infirmities? I believe that outside professional help
in organizing is the best answer. In the continuation of Mr. Rodwell's
remarks, he pays tribute to the usefulness of the Industrial Areas
Foundation. What he says applies to all five ways community organizations get stuck: "The IAF helps us survive those internal
troubles before they get hot."

It's not just a need for one-time troubleshooters who can be called
in at a critical time. When Dolores Martinez credits the Organize
Training Center with being "instrumental" in MOP's development,
she emphasizes that "they've been with us through the evolution
of our organization." That longevity is what gives the relationship
between a community organization and an outside organizing program its mutual trust, its understanding, its effectiveness. It's a relationship I believe is exceedingly valuable for the development of
a strong, responsible community organization.

I haven't come easily to this conclusion. I guess I wish it weren't
true; I wish community organizations could just make it on their
own. But it doesn't seem to happen that way. In the communities
where we are the most eager to see organizations grow, there are
too many liabilities, too many hazards, too little margin for error.
One leader once remarked dolefully during a troubled time, "We've
got almost as many potholes in this organization as there are out
there in our streets."

Both the IAF and the OTC are small clusters of experienced,
thoughtful people in organizing. So is the Gamaliel Foundation,
the new program coming out of the UNO experience in Chicago.
These and a few others like them (see app. I) specialize in long-
term contractual relationships with community organizations. They

are certainly useful in the beginning; indeed, they have taken initiatives to start community organizations. But their value becomes
even greater as organizations mature. They know their clients or
affiliates well and vice versa. After awhile, like all good consultants, there's not much a center can tell its community organization client that the client doesn't know already, but the center should
be respected enough to be able to help the leaders and staff keep
looking at themselves honestly and constructively. A center performing that role well can make the difference between stability
and chaos, usefulness and uselessness.

Moreover, the greatest value of these centers may not be in their
one-on-one relationships with community groups but rather in the
way they bring together people from the various organizations with
which they work. Parochialism is a natural enemy of good community organizing; leaders and staff of different organizations gain
a great deal when they struggle with concepts together at training
sessions, or collaborate on some activity of joint concern.

In the face of the five midlife organizational crises just identified, these organizing centers can (1) challenge leaders to give top
priority to bringing along a lot of other leaders, (2) sound the alarm
about disorderliness and show how other organizations cope, (3)
keep pushing for community efforts that aren't a waste of time,
(4) keep making the point that the organization will be just part
of the problem if the leadership can't find ways to organize some
good times in the neighborhood for everyone including themselves,
and (5) butt in when an organization is all turned in on itself with
internal struggles and ask whether that's what the people involved
really want to do or whether they want to help the community.

As Ms. Martinez says, "They [OTC] are great on stress. . . . They
keep asking us over and over again what's important to us, what
our values are."

Of course, there are potential dangers when a community group
is an affiliate of an outside resource. It can lose its independence,
becoming co-opted and used for somebody else's purposes instead
of its own. It can become just a dependent part of some larger coalition or development program that uses the group as one of its
tokens of accountability to the community. The organization's leaders must be strong to stay in charge and keep the organization accountable to the community rather than to any outside organizing

program. It's up to them to keep their organization's prime attention on its neighborhood roots and maintain the open, inclusive, patient stance that will keep those roots healthy and growing. The experiences so far of BUILD, MOP, and UNO show it can be done. Mr. Rodwell really means it when he says BUILD would fire the IAF anytime it seemed to outlive its usefulness. Unlike the relationships we may be more accustomed to seeing between not-for-profit organizations and outside experts, the contracts between these community organizations and organizing centers tend to be between equal parties. If there's to be any value to the relationship at all, the community organization is a strong client and—more than a client—a strong, influential affiliate of the organizing center along with other community organizations.

The provisions of the contracts vary. At BUILD, as noted previously, the organization pays IAF for its staff direction and a continuing program of leadership training. MOP purchases training and consulting time from OTC. UNO of Chicago does approximately the same with Gamaliel and gets some valuable trainee placements. There are many alternatives, depending on an organization's stage of development, the outside resources it needs for its own stability and growth, and the ideas for joint activities that emerge from contacts with other organizations through the organizing center.

It behooves a donor interested in this field to see what relationships already exist between local community organizations and such organizing centers as these, and to judge what affect they are having. If such relationships don't exist, the contributor or potential contributor can join with interested community groups or leaders to explore whatever initial conversations seem appropriate.

It's an exciting time for funders to be close to community organizations. Largely through the leadership of the IAF, the 1980s have seen a reaffirmation of the importance of a strong base for an organization. The term *church-based* organizing has come into common usage, referring to an intensive process that helps a congregation "act upon its faith" in its own parish and then in the larger community. For BUILD, MOP, UNO, and organizations like them, the style becomes more accurately called *institution-based organizing*, with a broad definition of *institution*. Churches are joined by neighborhood groups, clusters of block clubs, parents organizations, community-based social service agencies, unions, chambers of commerce, and other kinds of self-help and social groups. As Mike Kromrey of MOP points out, the member institutions and organizations by no means belong to the larger organization. A better clarity seems to exist today about the inevitable, creative tensions between the need for these strong autonomous parts and the insistence that they add up to an organization of sufficient scale to address the important issues of the community. The insights we have about institution-based organizing have made it easier to work with the difficult fact that community organizations have to think small and big at the same time.

But there are always new ideas, new designs, new accommodations to conditions. For instance, chapter 5 showed the current emphasis on self-responsibility among neighborhood institutions and their leaders to do their own staffing for neighborhood organizing, and the consequent cuts in community organization staffs. It has been a time to stress volunteers and to establish a higher level of professionalism (and pay) for the staff positions that remain. But given how much is now expected of leaders and staff in these organizations, it's not hard to predict that the pendulum may swing back, and more staffing—maybe new types of jobs with new job descriptions—will be seen as needed. That could be especially true in some of the poorest communities, where there aren't as many indigenous institutions strong enough to assume the initial responsibilities in organizing. Whether such staff expansion can be seriously considered, of course, will partly depend on whether there are funding sources that understand and value the opportunities to invest in community organizations.

There are changes in issues, too. At present, the years of attention to the troubles of public school systems seem to be culminating in dramatic new approaches that place community groups at the heart of movements to reorganize the schools to be effective for children. At the same time, organizations such as UNO in Chicago are beginning to figure out more effective roles in the economic development activity of their larger communities and metropolitan areas, and that field looks likely to become the next major focus of program development among leading community groups. The prospect of bonafide community organizations finding ways to enable people in poor communities to identify what their own resources are and how they can be productive within the larger economy is an exciting one worth encouraging.

In any case, the character of community organizing being forged by the likes of BUILD, MOP, and UNO and their outside sources of training and counsel is one that renders such funding opportunities more attractive than ever. Much importance is placed on stability, on having the roots of an organization deep and broad enough to withstand troubles and allow members to address community needs with enough staying power to get something accomplished. That makes for a good philanthropic investment.

Chapter 11

CONCLUSION:
THE NEED TO TRUST THE PUBLIC

If for the moment you eliminate some personal motivations like getting tax breaks and impressing people and gaining immortality, there are really only three basic reasons for giving away money:

(1) *To solve problems.* You want to identify important problems and needs, determine ways to get at them that make sense, and then put your money on those prescribed solutions. You know some will work and some won't, but you want to be part of the exciting philanthropic tradition of directly funding specific new approaches you're convinced have merit and promise.

(2) *To strengthen institutions*, with a broad enough definition of *institution* to include all kinds of organizations and agencies. Rather than deal so directly with problem solving, you figure it's better—in your case at least—to help put in place the institutions that can solve the problems and meet the needs of our society as they arise. You visualize a map or a model of our society's landscape, showing these institutions strategically placed, serving their constituencies, representing enlightenment and integrity, and becoming—with your help—enormously valuable assets to the community.

(3) *To build the public life of the community.* You don't presume to know enough about problems to support single, specific solutions, and you've seen a lot of institutions come and go, rise and fall. You're more inclined to leave it to the people of a community and the nation to develop their own institutions and try to solve their own problems, and you want to invest in enhancing their abilities to do so.

All three approaches to the tasks of philanthropy are good and proper. The first does indeed have a distinguished history of direct accomplishment, whether it's the cure for a disease or the timely funding of an attractive new youth program in a neighborhood with troubled teenagers. The second is most appropriate for a great many donors, who learn how to recognize a good institution when they see one and give it the support it needs to maintain its services, grow, maybe have some constructive influence on other institutions, and tackle some of the community's problems it sees in the lives of people around it. The last is the least pursued of the three and, of course, it's been the aim of this book to help change that situation.

It should be noted that there are overlaps. Under my broad definition, and especially with today's emphasis on institution-based organizing and stability, community organizations are institutions. Furthermore, their members are often neighborhood-based institutions, which gain as much as they give in their relationships with good community organizations. So you are strengthening institutions, helping them get positioned firmly in the right places on your map of the territory, when you support community organizations to accomplish the third objective.

A couple of concluding things can be said in the context of this list of three. First, it's clear that in the third category we're talking about *local* philanthropy. National foundations and fund drives can give to cures and find institutions to support, even local ones, but they show great difficulty in getting close enough to society to invest in cultivating our public life. The realities of our coping with one another are played out in small arenas. The actual practice of democracy comes alive and gets defined in local settings. As John Dewey told us, *"Only when we start from a community as a fact*, grasp the fact in thought so as to clarify and enhance its constituent elements, *can we reach an idea of democracy which is not utopian*[emphasis added]."

The *"community as a fact"* becomes the place where local philanthropy can find its lively opportunities to give.

Second, those who aspire to the third choice are making a statement about who they feel should be in charge of people's lives and institutions and problem-solving processes. The people themselves must define needs and invent solutions. Jane Jacobs, the grand urban teller of tales, says in her new book that if we've learned anything about fixing our cities, it's that community development can't be given; it's something that has to be *done*. If that's the case, then we have only two choices: we can decide that nothing can be done, or we can learn to trust the public more than most philanthropy seems now to do. That's an important function of community organizations. BUILD, MOP, UNO, and others, and leaders such as the ones this book has quoted, can help us learn how much a group of citizens can do when given a chance to put together an effective instrument for community voice and action.

Note that the public doesn't mean the teaming millions or everyone watching television. It means the public realm, the common public life, in which people get together both in small clusters and in those broader, increasingly comprehensive communities, to work out part of their lives together. Improving the chances for this to happen by supporting community organizations is a philanthropic assertion of a trust in the public. It affirms and nourishes the vitality of all those circles of community on which we depend. Emphasizing the deliberate action involved, sociobiologist Harvey Wheeler calls this type of deed "*intentional* altruism." Our troubles are man-made; we can overcome them. That's the Spirit of '76.

In this book we began by establishing the necessities of citizen participation in how our country is run and by looking at the ways in which these necessities have not been secured. Part I concluded with a set of specifications for programs to enhance participation and identified community organizations as at least one important type of resource that meets these specifications. Part II has talked about the philanthropic response to this opportunity from several viewpoints, ranging from Italian history and sociobiology to the nuts and bolts of how to make grants and how to help advance the skills and strengths of community organization work.

We have been following the trail of Robert Dahl since chapter 2, and it's fitting to finish with his more recent thoughts. He says that to prevail over the difficulties of pluralism we need to search for

> mutually beneficial and mutually acceptable outcomes, . . .
> but unless we are told what political processes and structures will increase the likelihood of discovering and bringing about such outcomes. . . , an exhortation to search for the common good does not take one very far.

My case here has been that effective community organizations indeed provide an important part of those key "processes and structures" and that they do lead to "mutually beneficial and mutually acceptable outcomes."

In the same article, after calculating the damages from increased centralization of power and control in our pluralistic society, Dahl concludes that it should make sense to adopt "an alternative strategy of decentralization, together with the democratization of relatively autonomous subsystems." But, he says, such a strategy is flawed because "the resources of the various subsystems are likely to vary." The whole thing won't work because communities have such different strengths. Communities of poor people don't have the built-in means to do what needs to be done.

That's exactly where private philanthropy can find its place, promoting participation and making grants to reduce the variance among those resources, so that all communities can contribute to the essential public life of our American democracy. Such a role deserves to become philanthropy's first charity.

The point was made in the description of BUILD and it applies to MOP, UNO, and a host of other good organizing experiences: success in solving our society's problems comes not just from bright ideas or from fresh blue-ribbon committees established overnight to address single issues. It comes from the involvement of broad-based community organizations that have been building constituencies, generating leadership, and working on a variety of community problems for a long enough time to have developed some skills in and insights into those complex activities. Such strengths have to have their roots in a lot of basic neighborhood organizing. It all takes time and ultimately depends on the vision and energies of the community people themselves. One of the only ways in which interested outsiders can help the process is by providing some of the enabling money required to let it happen. The offer of these funds, and the experience necessary to give them well, has to begin now.

Appendix I

Sources of Assistance to Community Organizations

There is a great range of services among these centers. A few—including the Industrial Areas Foundation, the Gamaliel Foundation, and the Organize Training Center, which work with the three organizations described in this book—specialize almost exclusively in long-term contractual relationships with community organizations, in the manner referred to in chapter 10. Others choose to concentrate on shorter-term consulting work or training sessions. Some provide help to other organizations while advancing active community programs of their own. A few have ties to community organizations in several sections of the country; others have a distinct local focus within a city, metropolitan area, state, or region.

Although they share a common basic interest in organizing, the centers represent a rich diversity of experiences and approaches. Recognizing this diversity, anyone inquiring about specific community organizations or the field in general would probably benefit from contacting at least two or three centers rather than just one.

I have not included the agencies that provide useful management assistance to community groups as well as to other not-for-profit organizations, but whose major interest and expertise is not in organizing itself.

There is little or no chance that this list is all-inclusive. Although I have checked around a good deal, I have very likely overlooked some valuable organizations, and I regret having done so.

Association of Community Organizations for Reform Now (ACORN)
1026 Elysian Fields Ave.
New Orleans, La. 70117
(504) 943-8994
Wade Rathke, chief organizer

Center for Community Action
149 Roxbury St.
Roxbury, Mass. 02119
(617) 445-7708
Chuck Turner, director

Center for Community Change
1000 Wisconsin Ave., N.W.
Washington, D.C. 20007
(202) 342-0519
Pablo Eisenberg, president
Don Leaming-Elmer, organizational development specialist

Center for Third World Organizing
4228 Telegraph Ave.
Oakland, Calif. 94609
(415) 654-9601
Gary Delgado, co-director

Direct Action and Research Training Center (DART)
137 N.E. 19th St.
Miami, Fla. 33132
(305) 576-8020
John Calkins, director
Holly Holcombe, associate director

Eastern Communities Training Institute
1164 S. 11th St.
Philadelphia, Pa. 19147
(215) 465-9688
Kathleen O'Toole, director
Steve Honeyman, associate director

The Gamaliel Foundation
220 S. State St.
Chicago, Ill. 60604
(312) 427-4616
Gregory A. Galluzzo, executive director

Grassroots Leadership, Inc.
P.O. Box 9586
Charlotte, N.C. 28299
(704) 332-3090
Si Kahn, executive director

Great Lakes Institute
2055 Marengo Dr.
Toledo, Ohio 43614
(419) 389-9766
David Beckwith, president

Highlander Research and Education Center
Route 3, Box 370, Russell Gap Rd.
New Market, Tenn. 37820
(615) 933-3443
Hubert Sapp, director

Industrial Areas Foundation
36 New Hyde Park Rd.
Franklin Square, N.Y. 11010
(516) 354-1076
Edward Chambers, executive director

Institute for Social Justice
523 West 15th St.
Little Rock, Ark. 72202
(501) 376-7153
Elena Hanggi, executive director

Maine Leadership Development
P.O. Box 17801
Portland, Maine 04101
(207) 874-1146
Marjorie Phyfe, director

Mid-America Institute
9401 South Leavitt Ave.
Chicago, Ill. 60620
(312) 779-9108
Thomas A. Gaudette, director

Midwest Academy
225 W. Ohio St.
Chicago, Ill. 60610
(312) 645-6010
Jackie Kendall, director

National Training and Information Center
810 N. Milwaukee Ave.
Chicago, Ill. 60622
(312) 243-3035
Gale Cincotta, executive director
Shel Trapp, staff director

Northern Rockies Action Group
9 Placer St.
Helena, Mont. 59601
(406) 442-6615
Michael D. Schechtman, executive director

Organizing and Leadership Training Center
169 Massachusetts Ave.
Boston, Mass. 02115
(617) 536-1200
Lewis Finfer, director

Organize Training Center
1095 Market St., #419
San Francisco, Calif. 94103
(415) 552-8990
Mike Miller, director

Pacific Institute for Community Organizations
171 Santa Rosa Ave.
Oakland, Calif. 94610
(415) 655-2801
John A. Baumann, S. J., executive director

Southern Empowerment Project
315 Ellis Ave.
Maryville, Tenn. 37801
(615) 984-6500
June Rostan, coordinator

United Connecticut Action for Neighborhoods
P.O. Box 6422
Hartford, Conn. 06106
(203) 522-9946
Alta Lash, director
Jack Mimnaugh, consultant

Washington Area Training Center
1323 Girard St., N.W.
Washington, D.C. 20016
(301) 277-7085
Robert Johnsen, director

Western Organization of Resource Councils
412 Stapleton Building
Billings, Mont. 59117
(406) 252-9672
Pat Sweeney, director

Working in Neighborhoods
740 Circle Ave.
Cincinnati, Ohio 45232
(513) 541-4109
Sister Barbara Busch, director

Appendix II

Grantmaking Associations and Resources

Council on Foundations, Inc.
1828 L. St., N.W.
Washington, D.C. 20036
(202) 466-6512
James A. Joseph, president
   ("a national membership association of over 1,000 independent,
   community, operating and public foundations, corporate grantmakers and trust companies")

National Network of Grantmakers
2000 P St., N.W., Ste. 410
Washington, D.C. 20036
(202) 822-9236
   ("an association of individuals involved in grantmaking who are
   committed to social and economic justice." Publishes an infor-
   mative directory.)

The Foundation Center
79 Fifth Ave.
New York, N.Y. 10003
(212) 620-4230
Thomas R. Buckman, president

and 1001 Connecticut Ave., N.W.
   Washington, D.C. 20036
   (202) 331-1400

312 Sutter St.
San Francisco, Calif. 94108
(415) 397-0902

1442 Hanna Building
1422 Euclid Ave.
Cleveland, Ohio 44115
(216) 861-1933

(the principal source of published information about the field, with libraries in the above offices and "cooperating collections" at many public, university, and foundation libraries in other cities)

Independent Sector
1828 L St., N.W.
Washington, D.C. 20036
(202) 223-8100
Brian O'Connell, president
(a coalition of voluntary organizations, foundations, and corporations interested in philanthropy and voluntary action)

Campaign for Human Development
United States Catholic Conference
1312 Massachusetts Ave., N.W.
Washington, D.C. 20005
(202) 659-6650

(a national program funding grass roots organizations and agencies in poor communities, with knowledgeable national and regional staff)

University Centers

The following five university centers are included as leading examples of university resources with considerable emphasis on research and information programs and strong interests in the field of grantmaking. Several other universities have established programs in not-for-profit management. Research and career development in this area is a growing field in higher education; inquiries at convenient universities might yield information about interesting new resources that would be useful to donors.

Program on Non-Profit Organizations
Institution for Social and Policy Studies
Yale University
P.O. Box 154, Yale Station
New Haven, Conn. 06520
(203) 432-2121
Melissa Middleton, associate director

Center for the Study of Philanthropy
Graduate School & University Center
City University of New York
33 West 42nd St.
New York, N.Y. 10036
(212) 642-2130
Kathleen D. McCarthy, director

Center for the Study of Philanthropy and Voluntarism
Institute of Policy Sciences and Public Affairs
Duke University
4875 Duke Station
Durham, N.C. 27706
(919) 684-2672
Charles T. Clotfelter, director

Indiana University Center on Philanthropy
850 W. Michigan St.
Indianapolis, Ind. 46223
(317) 274-4200
Howard Schaller, acting director

The Mandel Center for Nonprofit Management
Case Western Reserve University
2035 Abington Ave.
Cleveland, Ohio 44106
(216) 368-2275
Dennis Young, director

Regional Associations of Grantmakers ("RAGs")
These regional and local associations vary a great deal in their programs and services, but all are useful in bringing together donors, board members, staff members, corporate representatives, and others involved in philanthropy.

Multistate Associations

Conference of Southwest Foundations
P.O. Box 8832
Corpus Christi, Texas 78412
(512) 850-5054
Maud W. Keeling, executive secretary

Pacific Northwest Grantmakers Forum
c/o The Seattle Foundation
425 Pike St., Ste. 510
Seattle, Wash. 98101
(206) 622-2294
Catherine Anstett, administrator

Southeastern Council on Foundations
134 Peachtree St., N.W.
Atlanta, Ga. 30303
(404) 524-0911
Robert H. Hull, president

State Associations

Associated Grantmakers of Massachusetts, Inc.
294 Washington St., Room 840
Boston, Mass. 02108
(617) 426-2606
Miguel Satut, president

Council of Michigan Foundations
P.O. Box 599
Grand Haven, Mich. 49417
(616) 842-7080
Dorothy A. Johnson, president

Council of New Jersey Grantmakers
57 Washington St.
East Orange, N.J. 07107
(201) 676-5905
Robert Corman, chair

Donors Forum of Ohio
c/o Bank One, Dayton, NA, Trust Dept.
Kettering Tower
Dayton, Ohio 45401
(513) 449-8963
Louis W. Feldmann, treasurer

Foundation Forum of Wisconsin
117 West Boundary Road
Mequon, Wis. 53092
(414) 241-3973
Connie Bach, executive director

Grantmakers of Western New York
c/o The Buffalo Foundation
237 Main St.
Buffalo, N.Y. 14203
(716) 852-2857
William L. Van Schoonhoven, president

Grantmakers of Western Pennsylvania
572 One Mellon Bank Center
Pittsburgh, Pa. 15258
(412) 234-0829
Kate Dewey, executive director

Indiana Donors Alliance
c/o The Indiana Committee for the Humanities
1500 North Delaware
Indianapolis, Ind. 46202
(317) 638-1500
Kenneth Gladish, secretary

Minnesota Council on Foundations
425 Peavey Building
Minneapolis, Minn. 55402
(612) 338-1989
Jacqueline Reis, president

Northern California Grantmakers
116 New Montgomery St.
San Francisco, Calif. 94105
(415) 777-5761
Caroline Tower, executive director

Southern California Association for Philanthropy
315 W. Ninth St., Ste. 1000
Los Angeles, Calif. 90015
(213) 489-7307
Lon M. Burns, president

Greater City Associations

Association of Baltimore Area Grantmakers
c/o Community Foundation of Greater Baltimore
6 East Hamilton St.
Baltimore, Md. 21202
(301) 332-4171
Martha Johnston, program officer

Clearinghouse for Midcontinent Foundations
P.O. Box 22680
Kansas City, Mo. 64113
(816) 276-1176
Linda H. Talbott, president

Co-ordinating Council for Foundations, Inc.
999 Asylum Ave.
Hartford, Conn. 06105
(203) 525-5585
Bertina Williams, executive director

Donors Forum of Chicago
53 W. Jackson Boulevard, Ste. 430
Chicago, Ill. 60604
(312) 431-0260
Valerie Lies, president

Grantmakers Forum
1456 Hanna Building
Cleveland, Ohio 44115
(216) 861-3810
Marjorie M. Carlson, program coordinator

Rochester Grantmakers Forum
c/o Wegman's Food Markets
1500 Brooks Ave., Box 844
Rochester, N.Y. 14692
(716) 464-4760
Mary Ellen Burris

New York Regional Association of Grantmakers
505 Eighth Ave., 18th Fl.
New York, N.Y. 10018
(212) 714-0699
Barbara Bryan, executive director

Metropolitan Association for Philanthropy
5585 Pershing Ave., Ste. 150
St. Louis, Mo. 63112
(314) 361-3900
Amy R. Rome, executive director

San Diego Grantmakers
c/o San Diego Community Foundation
525 B St., Ste. 410
San Diego, Calif. 92101
(619) 239-8815
Pamela Hall

Donors Forum of Miami
200 S. Biscayne, Ste. 3480
Miami, Fla. 33122
Marilyn Gladstone, executive director

BIBLIOGRAPHY

This becomes an unusual mix. It's interesting to see what a broad variety of ideas impinge upon philanthropy.

All these sources are referred to in the text or footnotes. We haven't had many bibliographies about subjects in philanthropy, so perhaps it's permissible to single out a few for separate comment.

Some works are obviously basic to the perspectives of this book, especially those of Robert Dahl, John Dewey, Mancur Olson, Kenneth Arrow, Hannah Arendt, and Thomas Jefferson (his letters).

Others are particularly distinguished, readable books, each of which has its own clear bearing on philanthropy—for instance, those by Paul Starr, Albert Hirschman, Peter Hall, David Rothman, Richard Trexler (and the rest of Frederic Jaher's book), Garrett Hardin, Russell Hardin, Kenneth Boulding, Joan Simpson Burns, and the four books referred to in a footnote about sociobiology (chap. 7).

Some of these may be new to us but famous in their primary fields. Paul Starr's *The Social Transformation of American Medicine* is a good example; it is a seminal work appreciated by a broad variety of people concerned about health care. (In 1984, Starr became the first sociologist to win a Pulitzer Prize.) Yet the fact that his wide-angle view happens to recognize and reflect a lot that is relevant to philanthropy is not generally noticed. Albert Hirschman, perhaps in other books more than the book noted here, approaches community affairs largely from work in developing countries; he brings provocative insights that are often as pertinent to philanthropy here as they are overseas. Peter Hall has acted upon his interest in private institutions and taken a step closer to us; he is presently with the Program on Nonprofit Organizations at Yale

University. Among these three and the rest listed and I'm sure a few more, we in philanthropy have more authors writing to us than we may sometimes imagine. They make good reading.

The references to journal articles deserve note. These are much more readily available in libraries than many of the books listed and are brief and specific.

Ad Hoc Funders' Committee for Voter Registration and Education. *Funders' Guide to Voter Registration and Education.* New York, 1983.

Amir, Shmuel, and David Bigman. "A Welfare Function of Altruism and its Biological Rationale." *Journal of Social and Biological Structures* 3 (January 1980): 55-66.

Andrews, Wayne. *Battle for Chicago.* New York: Harcourt Brace, 1946.

Arendt, Hannah. *The Human Condition.* Chicago: University of Chicago Press, 1958.

Arrow, Kenneth. *Social Choice and Individual Values.* 2d ed. New York: John Wiley, 1963.

Barash, David P. *Sociobiology and Behavior.* 2d ed. New York: Elsevier, 1982.

Barry, Brian. "Circumstances of Justice and Future Generations." In *Obligations to Future Generations*, edited by R. I. Sikora and Brian Barry. Philadelphia: Temple University Press, 1978.

_____ . *Sociologists, Economists and Democracy.* London: Collier McMillan, 1970.

Barry, Brian, and Russell Hardin. *Rational Man and Irrational Society?* Beverly Hills, Calif.: Sage, 1982.

Batchelder, Alan B. *Economics of Poverty.* 2d ed. New York: John Wiley, 1971.

Benson, C. Randolph. *Thomas Jefferson as a Social Scientist.* Cranberry, N.J.: Fairleigh Dickinson University Press, 1971.

Berelson, Bernard R., Paul F. Lazarsfeld, and William N. McPhee. *Voting.* Chicago: University of Chicago Press, 1954.

Boorstin, Daniel J., ed. *The American Primer.* Chicago: University of Chicago Press, 1966.

_____ , *The Americans.* Vol. 1, *The Colonial Experience.* New York: Random House, 1958.

Boulding, Kenneth E. Review of *The Political Economy of Change*, by Warren F. Ilchman and Norman Thomas Uphoff. *American Political Science Review* 64 (1970): 603.

Boulding, Kenneth E. and Martin Pfaff. "Future Directions." In *Redistribution to the Rich and the Poor: The Grants Economy of Income*

Distribution, edited by Boulding and Pfaff, 387-390. Belmont, Calif.: Wordsworth, 1972.

Boyd, Julian P., ed. *The Papers of Thomas Jefferson*, Princeton, N.J.: Princeton University Press, 1954.

Bureau of the Census. *Current Population Reports*, ser P-20, nos. 397 and 414. Washington, D.C.: GPO.

Burnham, Walter Dean. "The Changing Shape of the American Political Universe." *American Political Science Review* 59 (March 1965): 7-28.

Burns, Joan Simpson. *The Awkward Embrace: The Creative Artist and the Institutions in America*. New York: Alfred A. Knopf, 1975.

Campbell, Angus, Philip E. Converse, Warren E. Miller, and Donald E. Stokes. *The American Voter*. Chicago: University of Chicago Press, 1960.

Carnegie Endowment for International Peace. *A Manual of the Carnegie Benefactions*. Washington, D.C.: 1919.

Charvet, John. *A Critique of Freedom and Equality*. New York: Cambridge University Press, 1981.

Cigler, Allan J., and Burdett A. Loomis, eds. *Interest Group Politics*. Washington, D.C.: CQ Press, 1983.

Cohen, Ronald. "Altruism: Human, Cultural, or What?" *Journal of Social Issues* 28, 3 (1972): 39-57.

Cole, Richard L. "Constituent Development in Non-Profit Organizations." Working paper of the Program on Nonprofit Organizations, Yale University, n.d.

Dahl, Robert A. "Comment on Manley." *American Political Science Review* 77 (June 1983): 386-388.

_____ . *Dilemmas of Pluralist Democracy: Autonomy vs. Control*. New Haven: Yale University Press, 1982.

_____ . "Further Reflections on 'The Elitist Theory of Democracy.' " *American Political Science Review* 60 (June 1966): 296-305.

_____ . "On Removing Certain Impediments to Democracy in the United States." *Political Science Quarterly* 92 (Spring 1977): 1-20.

_____ . "Pluralism Revisited." *Comparative Politics* 10 (January 1978): 191-203.

_____ . *Who Governs? Democracy and Power in an American City*. New Haven: Yale University Press, 1961.

Dawkins, Richard. *The Selfish Gene*. New York: Oxford, 1976.

Dewey, John. *Liberalism and Social Action*. 1935. Reprint. New York: G.P. Putnam, 1963.

_____ . *The Public and Its Problems*. 1927. Reprint. Chicago: Gateway Books, 1946.

Drotning, Phillip. "Thoughts of a Corporate Gadfly." Donors Forum of Chicago, *Forum* (Winter 1984).

Easton, David. "The New Revolution in Political Science." *American Political Science Review* 63 (December 1969): 1051-1061.

Embree, Edwin Rogers, and Julia Waxman. *Investment in People: The Story of the Julius Rosenwald Fund*. New York: Harper, 1949.

Eulau, Heinz. "Skill Revolution and Consultative Commonwealth." *American Political Science Review* 67 (March 1973): 169-191.

Ford Foundation. Annual Reports, 1965 and 1966. New York.

_____ . "Finances of the Performing Arts." New York, 1974.

Freeman, David F. *The Handbook on Private Foundations*. Washington, D.C.: Seven Locks Press, 1981.

Gaus, Gerald F. *The Modern Liberal Theory of Man*. New York: St. Martin's Press, 1983.

Gaylin, Willard, Ira Glasser, Steven Marcus, and David Rothman. *Doing Good: The Limits of Benevolence*. New York: Pantheon Press, 1978.

Grantsmanship Center. *Program Planning & Proposal Writing*. Los Angeles, 1980.

Greenstone, J. David, and Paul E. Peterson. *Race and Authority in Urban Politics*. New York: Russell Sage Foundation, 1973.

Gregory, Michael S., Anita Silvers, and Diane Sutch, eds. *Sociobiology and Human Nature*. San Francisco: Jossey-Bass, 1978.

Hall, Peter Dobkin. *The Organization of American Culture, 1700–1900*. New York: New York University Press, 1982.

Hands, A.R. *Charities and Social Aid in Greece and Rome*. Ithaca, N.Y.: Cornell University Press, 1968.

Hardin, Garrett. *The Limits of Altruism*. Bloomington: Indiana University Press, 1977.

Hardin, Russell. *Collective Action*. Baltimore, Md.: Johns Hopkins University Press, 1982.

Heale, M. J. "Humanitarianism in the Early Republic: The Moral Reformers of New York, 1776–1825." *Journal of American Studies* 2 (October 1968): 161-175.

Hertzlinger, Regina, and William Krasker. "Who Profits from Non-Profits?" *Harvard Business Review* 65 (January/February 1987): 93-106.

Hirschman, Albert O. *Shifting Involvements: Private Interest and Public Action*. Princeton, N.J.: Princeton University Press, 1982.

The Holy Bible. Rev. standard version. New York: Thomas Nelson, 1952.

Hunter, Floyd. *Community Power Structure*. Chapel Hill: University of North Carolina Press, 1953.

_____ . *Community Power Succession: Atlanta's Policy-Makers Revisited*. Chapel Hill: University of North Carolina Press, 1980.

Ingram, Helen M., Nancy K. Laney, and John R. McCain. *A Policy Approach to Political Representation: Lessons from the Four Corners States*. Baltimore, Md.: Johns Hopkins University Press, 1980.

Jacobs, Jane. *Cities and the Wealth of Nations: Principles of Economic Life*. New York: Random House, 1984.

Joseph, James A. "Preface." In *Community Leadership and Organized Philanthropy*. Washington, D.C.: Council on Foundations, 1986.

_____. "Testimony of James A. Joseph, President, Council on Foundations, at Hearings before House Subcommittee on Oversight, Committee on Ways and Means, June 27, 1983." Washington, D.C.: Council on Foundations.

Karl, Barry D. "Philanthraphobia in American History." Mimeographed copy of an address, 24 October 1982.

Kesselman, Mark. "The Conflictual Evolution of American Political Science: From Apologetic Pluralism to Trilateralism and Marxism." In *Public Values and Private Power in American Politics*, edited by J. David Greenstone, 34-67. Chicago: University of Chicago Press, 1982.

Key, V.O., Jr. *The Responsible Electorate*. Cambridge: Harvard University Press, 1966.

Layzer, David. "Altruism and Natural Selection." *Journal of Social and Biological Structures* 1 (July 1978): 297-305.

Lindeman, Eduard C. *Wealth and Culture*. New York: Harcourt, Brace, 1936.

Lindsay, A.D. *Essentials of Democracy*. 1929. Reprint. New York: Oxford University Press, 1948.

Lipset, Seymour Martin. *Political Man: The Social Bases of Politics*. Garden City, N.Y.: Doubleday, 1960.

_____. "Radicalism or Reformism: The Sources of Working Class Politics." *American Political Science Review* 77 (March 1983): 1-18.

Lowi, Theodore J. *The End of Liberalism*. New York: W.W. Norton, 1969.

Lynd, Robert S., and Helen M. Lynd. *Middletown*. New York: Harcourt, Brace, 1929.

_____. *Middletown in Transition*. New York: Harcourt, Brace, 1937.

Macpherson, C.B. *The Life and Times of Liberal Democracy*. Oxford: Oxford University Press, 1977.

_____. *The Real World of Democracy*. Oxford: Clarendon Press, 1966.

Malone, Dumas. *Jefferson and His Time*. Boston: Little, Brown, 1948.

Manley, John F. "Neo-Pluralism: A Class Analysis of Pluralism I and Pluralism II." *American Political Science Review* 77 (June 1983): 368-383.

Margolis, Howard. *Selfishness, Altruism and Rationality*. Cambridge: Cambridge University Press, 1982.

Maslow, Abraham H. *Motivation and Personality*. New York: Harper, 1954.

Mayer, Martin. *Bricks, Mortar and the Performing Arts*. New York: Twentieth Century Fund, 1970.

McCarthy, Kathleen D. *Noblesse Oblige: Charity and Cultural Philosophy in Chicago, 1849–1929*. Chicago: University of Chicago Press, 1982.

McKnight, John L. "The Future of Low-Income Neighborhoods and the People Who Reside There: A Capacity-Oriented Strategy for Neighborhood Development." Commissioned by the Charles Stewart Mott Foundation. Evanston, Ill.: Center for Urban Affairs and Policy Research, Northwestern University, 1987.

Melling, John Kennedy. *Discovering London's Guilds and Liveries*. London: Aylesbury-Shire Press, 1973.

Merelman, Richard M. "On the Neo-Elitist Critique of Community Power." *American Political Science Review* 62 (June 1969): 451-460.

Milbrath, Lester W. *Political Participation*. Chicago: Rand McNally, 1965.

Mill, John Stuart. *On Liberty* [1859]. Reproduced in *Utilitarianism, Liberty and Representative Government*. New York: E.P. Dutton, 1951.

Mills, C. Wright. *The Power Elite*. New York: Oxford University Press, 1956.

Milo, Ronald D. *Egoism and Altruism*. Belmont, Calif.: Wadsworth, 1973.

Moe, Terry M. *The Organization of Interests: Incentives and the Internal Dynamics of Political Interest Groups*. Chicago: University of Chicago Press, 1980.

Mussen, Paul, and Nancy Eisenberg-Berg. *Roots of Caring, Sharing and Helping: The Development of Prosocial Behavior in Children*. San Francisco: W.H. Freeman, 1977.

Nagel, Thomas. *The Possibility of Altruism*. Oxford: Clarendon Press, 1970.

Nason, John W. *Trustees and the Future of Foundations*. Washington, D.C.: Council on Foundations, 1977.

New World Foundation. *Initiatives for Community Self-Help: Efforts to Increase Recognition and Support*. New York, 1980.

Odendahl, Teresa. *America's Wealthy and the Future of Foundations*. New York: The Foundation Center, 1987.

O'Hare, William. "The Eight Myths of Poverty." *American Demographics* 8 (May 1986): 22-25

Olson, Mancur. *The Logic of Collective Action: Public Theory and the Theory of Groups*. Cambridge: Harvard University Press, 1965.

_____ . *The Rise and Decline of Nations: Economic Growth, Stag-flation and Social Rigidities*. New Haven: Yale University Press, 1982.

Padover, Saul K., ed. *The Complete Jefferson*. New York: Duell Sloan & Pearce, 1943.

_____ , ed. *Democracy: By Thomas Jefferson*. New York: Appleton-Century, 1939.

Pennock, J. Roland. *Democratic Political Theory*. Princeton, N.J.: Princeton University Press, 1979.

Pocincki, Leon, Stuart Dogger, and Barbara Schwartz. "Report of the Secretary's Commission on Medical Malpractice." U.S. Department of Health, Education and Welfare, 16 January 1973, 50-70.

Polsby, Nelson. *Community Power and Political Theory*. 1963. Reprint. New Haven: Yale University Press, 1980.

Pomper, Gerald M. "From Confusion to Clarity: Issues and American Voters, 1956–1968." *American Political Science Review* 66 (June 1972): 415-428.

RePass, David. "Issue Salience and Party Choice." *American Political Science Review* 65 (June 1971): 389-400.

Riker, William H. *Liberalism Against Populism: A Confrontation Between the Theory of Democracy and the Theory of Social Choice*. San Francisco: W.H. Freeman, 1982.

Rogin, Michael Paul. *The Intellectuals and McCarthy: The Radical Spector*. Cambridge: Massachusetts Institute of Technology Press, 1967.

Rothman, David J. *The Discovery of the Asylum*. Boston: Little, Brown, 1971.

Rousseau, Jean-Jacques. *The Social Contract; or, Principles of Political Right* [1762]. New York: New American Library, 1974.

Salisbury, Robert H. "Interest Representation: The Dominance of Institutions." *American Political Science Review* 78 (March 1984): 64-76.

Schumpeter, Joseph A. *Capitalism, Socialism and Democracy*. London: Allen and Unwin, 1943.

Silver, Morris. *Affluence, Altruism and Atrophy*. New York: New York University Press, 1980.

Simon, John G. "Foundations and Public Controversy." In *Future of Foundations*, edited by Fritz F. Heimann, 58-100. Englewood Cliffs, N.J.: Prentice-Hall, 1973.

Smith, David G. "Professional Responsibility and Political Participation." In *NOMOS* 16, *Participation in Politics*, edited by J. Roland Pennock and John W. Chapman, 213-232. New York: Lieber-Atherton, 1975.

Starr, Paul. *The Social Transformation of American Medicine*. New York: Basic Books, 1982.

Staub, Erwin. "Instigation to Goodness: The Role of Social Norms and

Interpersonal Influence." *Journal of Social Issues* 28, 3 (1972): 131-147.

Tocqueville, Alexis de. *Democracy in America* [1835]. New York: Alfred A. Knopf, 1945.

Trexler, Richard C. "Charity and the Defense of Urban Elites in the Italian Communes." In *The Rich, the Well Born, and the Powerful: Elites and Upper Classes in History*, edited by Frederic Cople Jaher, 64-109. Urbana: University of Illinois Press, 1973.

Troyer, Thomas A. "Can Foundations Support Voter Registration?" In *Foundation News* (November/December 1983): 22-23.

Truman, David B. "The American System in Crisis." *Political Science Quarterly* 74 (December 1959): 481-497.

Tullock, Gordon. "The Charity of the Uncharitable." *Western Economic Journal* (December 1971): 379-392. Also, in slightly different form, in Armen A. Alchian et al., eds., *The Economics of Charity*, 16-32. Old Woking, England: Gresham Press, 1973.

Verba, Sidney, and Norman H. Nie. *Participation in America: Political Democracy and Social Equality*. New York: Harper & Row, 1972.

Vickrey, William S. "One Economist's View of Philanthropy." In *Philanthropy and Public Policy*, edited by Frank G. Dickinson, 31-56. New York: National Bureau of Economic Research, 1962.

Walker, Jack L. "A Critique of the Elitist Theory of Democracy." *American Political Science Review* 60 (June 1966): 285-295.

Washington, H.A., ed. *Writings of Thomas Jefferson*. New York: John C. Riker, 1854.

Wheeler, Harvey. "Human Sociobiology: An Exploratory Essay." *Journal of Social and Biological Structures* 1 (October 1978): 307-318.

White, Elliott, ed. *Sociobiology and Human Politics*. Lexington, Mass.: Lexington Books, 1981.

Wilson, Edward O. *Sociobiology*. Cambridge: Harvard University Press, 1975.

Wilson, Graham K. *Interest Groups in the United States*. Oxford: Clarendon Press, 1981.

Wilson, R. Jackson. *In Quest of Community: Social Philosophy in the United States, 1860-1920*. New York: John Wiley, 1968.

Wispé, Lauren. "Positive Forms of Social Behavior: An Overview." *Journal of Social Issues* 28, 3 (1972): 1-19.

Wolin, Sheldon. *Politics and Vision: Continuity and Innovation in Western Political Thought*. Boston: Little, Brown, 1960.

Woodson, Robert L. "The Importance of Neighborhood Organizations in Meeting Human Needs." In *Meeting Human Needs: Towards a New Public Philosophy*, edited by Jack A. Meyer., 132-149. Washington, D.C.: American Enterprise Institute for Public Policy Research, 1982.

Wright, Derek S. *Psychology of Moral Behavior.* Baltimore, Md.: Penguin, 1971.

Yates, Douglas. *The Ungovernable City.* Cambridge: Massachusetts Institute of Technology Press, 1977.

Ylvisaker, Paul N. "Philanthropy as Triage." Paper presented to the community foundation subcommittee, Monterey, Calif., 2 October 1981.

Footnotes

(Works cited are listed in the bibliography.)

Introduction

page xv—"Our *well-wishing* can be unlimited": in Ronald D. Milo, p. 67.

page xviii—"I for one": John Dewey (1935), p. 92.

Chapter 1: The Promise of Participation

page 3—"Spirit of '76." Letter to Thomas Lomax, 12 March 1799, in H. A. Washington, ed., vol. 4, p. 300.

page 4—"loaded with misery by kings": Letter to George Wythe, 13 August 1786, in Julian P. Boyd, ed., vol. 10, pp. 244-245.

page 4—"Every government degenerates": Notes on Virginia, 1785, Query 14, in Saul K. Padover, ed. (1943), p. 668.

page 4—"I know of no safe depository": Letter to Charles Jarvis, 1821, in Saul K. Padover, ed. (1939), p. 138.

page 5—"We must delight in each other": Reproduced in Daniel J. Boorstin, ed. (1966), pt. 1, p. 22. Spelling has been modernized to conform with same passage quoted in R. Jackson Wilson, p. 1.

page 5—"When your mind shall be well improved": Letter to Peter Carr, 19 August 1785, in Boyd, ed., vol. 8, pp. 405-406.

page 5—"personal ambition should be a prudent admixture": Daniel J. Boorstin (1958), p. 142. Boorstin also points out that "your country" meant to Jefferson the State of Virginia as much or more as it meant the United States. Jefferson, says Boorstin, valued "the identity of the public man with the interests of his particular place."

page 6—"for it is a true rule": John Winthrop, in Boorstin, ed. (1966), p. 20.

page 6—Jean-Jacques Rousseau. See, for instance, Rousseau, bk. 2, chap. 4, pp. 47-53.

page 6—"ready-made, already processed": Dewey (1935), p. 39. C. Randolph Benson calls Jefferson's outlook pre-Darwinian," i.e., based on assumptions that man has a constant, unchangeable nature.

page 6—"boisterous sea of liberty": Letter to Philip Mazzei, 24 April 1796, in Washington, ed., vol. 4, p. 139.

page 6—"turbulence" of democracy, which "nourishes": Letter to James Madison, 30 January 1787, in Boyd, ed., vol. 11, p. 93.

page 7—If citizens were "not enlightened enough": Letter to Charles Jarvis, 1821, in Padover, ed. (1939), p. 138.

page 7—"I believe that all education proceeds by the participation of the individual": Reproduced in Boorstin (1966), pt. 2, pp. 609-611.

page 7—"Democracy is a name for a life of free and enriching communion": John Dewey (1927), p. 184. The claim made here that the invigorating qualities of community participation weren't emphasized until the late 1800s seems true within the context of our own U.S. political history. In a broader context there certainly were antecedents. In ancient Greece the stimulating effects of politics were valued highly. Between the eras of Jefferson and Dewey, John Stuart Mill wrote about the merits of participation as "the peculiar training of a citizen, the practical part of the political education of a free people, taking them out of the narrow circle of personal and family selfishness, and accustoming them to the comprehension of joint interests, the management of joint concerns—habituating them to act from public or semipublic motives and guide their conduct by aims which unite instead of isolating them from one another" (p. 222). But despite such insights about participation, Mill's qualifications as a democrat are questionable. He believed, for instance, in plural voting—i.e., in those citizens with superior qualifications being permitted to cast more votes than others.

For a recent analysis of "developmental democracy" (in contrast to "protective democracy") as viewed by Dewey, Mill, and others, see Gerald F. Gaus, chap. 6, esp. pp. 204-213.

page 8—to do otherwise would be to "set as zeroes": Letter to duPont de Nemours, 24 April 1816, in Washington, ed., vol. 6, p. 590. Jefferson was criticizing de Nemours's own designs for government, which would enfranchise property owners only. The revision in the Declaration of

Independence is discussed in Malone, vol. 1, pp. 227-228: the "Declaration and Resolves" of the Continental Congress in 1774 had described colonists' rights as being to "life, liberty and property."

Happiness had a special meaning at the time. Instead of just the very private, personal connotation of lightheartedness it has for us today, it also referred in liberal European traditions to a public happiness, a condition of shared well-being among members of a community. Albert O. Hirschman points out an interesting example: "la science du bonheur public" (the science of public happiness) was once a traditional name for the branch of knowledge that became "political economy" and then later, economics (p. 122).

page 9—"the second grade of purity": Letter to I. H. Tiffany, 26 August 1816, in Washington, ed., vol. 7, p. 32.

page 9—"from fear of the reticence of the national legislature": In Boorstin, ed. (1966), pt. 1, p. 131.

page 9—In practice there has always been attention to the positive nature: For a recent persuasive study that describes some of our better behavior as citizens and politicians, see Helen M. Ingram et al.

Chapter 2: The Prevailing Spell of Pluralism

page 11—Pluralism, as a description of how we act, is a product of the behavioralist approach to the social sciences, which has so radically changed our view of political science and other disciplines. Political science used to be the study of the state from the top down, concentrating on models of philosophy and structure—the Greeks, Marx, monarchies, etc. With today's interest in patterns of human behavior, much of political science focuses attention on how citizens act and think.

In the social sciences, behavioralism has been an extremely popular development because it yields opportunities for scientific methods in research and theoretical work akin to those of the natural sciences. Behavioralism in the social sciences is not to be confused with "behaviorism," the study of psychological response and the reinforcement of behavioral patterns developed by B.F. Skinner and others.

page 13—"is the enormous fly-wheel of society": Quoted in Dewey (1927), p. 159.

page 13—a "system dominated by many different sets of leaders": Robert Dahl (1961), p. 86. See also, for instance, pp. 227-228, 245, 314-316.

page 15—"What I am asserting": C. Wright Mills, p. 28.

page 15—but many of their peers: Nelson Polsby's *Community Power and Political Theory* is a critique of stratification theories about community power, such as those of Hunter and Mill and the Lynds, from a pluralist point of view. For brief examples of similar criticism, see David B. Truman, p. 487, and Mark Kesselman, p. 38. For later comment on how pluralist theory was initially a social science response to "power elite" conceptions, see Richard M. Merelman; and J. David Greenstone and Paul E. Peterson, p. 7.

page 17—they moved virtually overnight: Economist Kenneth E. Boulding, in his usual pungent style, calls this "invasion" an act of " 'economic imperialism,' that is, the attempt on the part of economics to take over all the other social sciences" (p. 603). For a good discussion of economic theory in the social sciences, see Brian Barry and Russell Hardin.

page 17—The basic economics assertion: For a convenient summary of Mancur Olson's logic, see his 1982 book, *The Risk and Decline of Nations*, chap. 2. For particularly clear, related insights, see Russell Hardin.

page 17—You can shake your finger and moralize at me: Social scientists who find Olson's ideas too confining have developed modifications, taking into account more of the guilt-responsibility-fear factors in human behavior and thereby softening the harshness of the economic model; see, for instance, Howard Margolis; and Terry M. Moe, chap. 5. The difficulty with these modified approaches, however, as the authors acknowledge, is that they immediately become infinitely reflective; they lose the sharp edges of Olson's theory. They have to deal in unmeasurables. According to Brian Barry (1970), "When we do allow for. . .altruism [as Margolis does], we must recognize that we weaken the deductive power of our economic model" (p. 23).

Russell Hardin points out that we are far from being able to construct an all-encompassing theory of human behavior; until we do, we need to recognize the limitations of admittedly narrower constructions such as Olson's but then use the insights they give us (p. 14).

page 18—free rider: The same good sense of the economic rational individual holds true for lots of other choices, including a familiar one in personal giving. When I get a mailing from an environmental reform agency asking for money, my decision whether to give is based on a lot of things besides my convictions about the importance of the cause and the merits of the agency. If that weren't the case, if all of us who tell pollsters we think environmental issues are important were actually to give to the cause, the budgets of agencies working on the problems would be many times what they are. But as it is, rationality will tell me—if my conscience lets it—that I really don't have to give. My ten or fifty dollars would be an imperceptible contribution that surely wouldn't make the difference between the agency's success or failure. If they succeed, I get just as much benefit (clean water or whatever) as someone who did give. If they fail, I haven't wasted my money. I'll take another look at the mailing in a day or two, but chances are a hundred to one that I'll be a free rider. One can be glad that so many of us overcome this logic and do give, but as Hardin remarks, compared with the seriousness of the issues confronted by such organizations, "the amount spent [and raised] is a trivium" (p. 11).

page 19—outcomes consistently fail: Barry and Hardin express Arrow's conclusion succinctly: "When preferences...of rational individuals are brought together, the outcome is collectively irrational" (p. 371).

page 19—Once upon a time the virtues of the American system: Compare Arrow's conclusion with an expression of the more conventional point of view that distrusts the individual but has faith in the society: "If the democratic system depended solely on the qualifications of the individual voter, then it seems remarkable that democracies have survived.... But when one considers...how the political system adjusts itself to changing conditions over long periods of time, he cannot fail to be impressed.... Where the rational citizen seems to abdicate, nevertheless angels seem to tread." Bernard R. Berelson et al., p. 311. Such a view is reminiscent of Adam Smith's "invisible hand." (Hannah Arendt had a quick word for such ideas about invisible hands and angels: "The invisible actor behind the scenes is an invention arising from a mental perplexity but corresponding to no real experience" [pp. 185-186].)
    Scholars have used Arrow's perceptions to help explain the incoherence and instability they see in politics. For a provocative example by a leading political scientist, see William H. Riker.

page 19—Dahl's people in New Haven: Processes described in *Who Governs?* (such as on p. 314) are like the picnic just discussed here. They yield, at best, an equilibrium of second choices.

pages 20-21—Quotations:

"There is an enormous mass of evidence": Robert Dahl (1966), p. 299.

"Individual voters seem unable": Berelson et al., p. 312.

"In general, people pay much less attention:" Angus Campbell et al., p. 182.

"The belief that a very high level of participation is always good": Seymour Martin Lipset (1960), p. 32.

page 21—Gallup poll results are referred to in Michael Paul Rogin, p. 232.

page 21—"Four years may not ordinarily": Truman, p. 495.

page 22—"hopeful expectations that were entertained": Hirschman, p. 13.

Chapter 3: Pluralism and the Promise of Participation

page 25—When we dwell on such destructive possibilities: A well-noted example of social scientists' concerns about the risks of social unrest is the one presented by Walter Dean Burnham, who concludes, "[T]he present situation perpetuates a standing danger that the half of the American electorate which is now more or less entirely outside the universe of active politics may someday be mobilized in substantial degree by totalitarian or quasi-totalitarian appeals" (p. 28).

page 26—Quotations:

"The local party leadership": Berelson et al., pp. 177-179.

"Party government. . . is today at a low ebb": (in the sense of parties having any control of government policies) J. Roland Pennock, p. 278.

"The whole paraphernalia of democratic procedures": Dahl (1961), p. 105.

page 26—"The world is a seamless web": Garrett Hardin (1977), p. 99.

page 27—"It reduces the numerous component decisions": Berelson et al., p. 183. Their reference is specifically to the American two-party system.

page 28—our task "is to temper the excesses of pluralism": Sheldon Wolin, p. 434. English political scientist John Charvet gives an especially forceful expression of the holistic perspective reacting to pluralism. In a chapter called "The Standpoint of the Whole," he recognizes that there will always be individual interests to be represented, "yet this does not mean that. . . instead of a common good there exists only a public arena in which conflicts of interest are fought out. This picture of political society contains, of course, an element of the truth, but the suggestion that it contains the whole truth is utterly destructive of community. Once the groups of civil society come to think in these terms, political society will soon be at an end. The standpoint of the whole involves the consideration of the claims of the different interests of civil society with a view to maintaining or altering the balance of the laws and institutions from the point of view, not of this or that interest, but of a conception of the long-run interest of the community. . . . Just as the individual develops himself as a free being in forming a conception of his life in terms of an ordering of values to be realized in it, so also must the community form a conception of its long-term identity in terms of an ordering of values that it seeks to realize. . . . It is by forming itself in accordance with such a self-conception that a community achieves its self-determination" (p. 189).

page 28—"How could a mass democracy work": Berelson et al., p. 314. Another leading interpreter of pluralism, Lester W. Milbrath, feels it is still necessary to affirm that active participation is a good thing, even if one is convinced to the contrary: "It is important to continue moral admonishment for citizens to become active in politics, not because we want or expect great masses of them to become active, but rather because the admonishment helps keep the system open and sustains a belief in the right of all to participate, which is an important norm governing the behavior of political elites" (p. 152). This posture has been called the "noble lie": Jack L. Walker, p. 287.

page 29—"Notables" in New Haven: Dahl (1961), pp. 78-79. As for nonparticipation among poor people, Sidney Verba and Norman H. Nie conclude from their research, "Those citizens with lower social status—low levels of education or income—are greatly overrepresented among those who are the inactives" (p. 97).

page 30—"[M]any leaders in the intervening structure": Truman, p. 489.

pages 31-32—"It is almost incredible": C.B. Macpherson (1966), p. 38.

Chapter 4: Specifications for New Activities

page 33—The pluralist description seems accurate enough: Although his recommendations for what to do about it are very different, Theodore J. Lowi describes pluralism in much the same way as I do here in chaps. 2 and 3, and he concludes that pluralism is "very much in line with the realities of modern life" (pp. 30-35).

C.B. Macpherson calls pluralism "equilibrium democracy" and says,

"As a description of the actual system now prevailing in Western liberal-democratic nations, [it] must be adjudged substantially accurate." His summary of pluralism's development is useful; as others do, he begins with the work of Joseph Schumpeter in 1942. C.B. Macpherson (1977), pp. 77-92.

One more terse related comment, from Hannah Arendt: "The trouble with modern theories of behavioralism is not that they are wrong but that they could become true, that they actually are the best possible conceptualization of certain obvious trends in modern society" (p. 322).

page 33—their leadership and a great majority of their active constituents: Lipset (1983), in his presidential address to the American Political Science Association, makes the point about the middle-class nature of the "post-materialist" movements involving "quality of life, sexual equality, ethnic rights, etc." (p. 16). In Allan J. Cigler and Burdett A. Loomis, eds. (1983), Andrew McFarland (pp. 340ff.) and Michael T. Hayes (pp. 113, 116) discuss the same phenomenon.

page 34—"Nothing is blinder": Dewey (1935), p. 56.

page 34—Interest groups continue to flourish: Data is from Robert H. Salisbury (1984), pp. 70-73. See also Salisbury in Cigler and Loomis, eds.: "The business sector is by a wide margin the largest and most complex area of group activity" (p. 360).

page 34—"Candidates don't have to go back": Quoted in Kenneth R. Clark, "Power for Sale," in *Chicago Tribune Magazine*, 27 April 1986.

page 34—Similar continued growth: *Chicago Tribune*, 16 June 1985, sec. 2, p. 1.

page 35—In the 1984 presidential election: 1984 and 1986 data are from Bureau of the Census, *Current Population Reports*, ser. P-20, nos. 397 and 414, respectively. Data about participation are too often, as they are here, limited to voting statistics because that's where the wealth of information is.

page 35—"voters seem to be acting more responsibly": David RePass, p. 400.

page 35—"Voters are not fools": V.O. Key, Jr., p. 7.

page 35—"found a substantial increase in ideological awareness": Gerald M. Pomper, p. 416.

page 36—"Black Americans have, in group consciousness": Verba and Nie, p. 173.

page 36—It finds that only 20 percent of us...[and] "Our data on the content of citizen-initiated contacts": Verba and Nie, pp. 31, 113.

page 36—"I disagree strongly": Dahl (1966), p. 103.

page 37—"In particular": Robert Dahl (1978), p. 199.

page 37—"stabilizing political inequalities": Robert Dahl (1982), pp. 40-47.

page 37—"for which no altogether satisfactory solution": Dahl (1978), p. 191. Dahl has proposed consideration of certain structural changes in government; see, for instance, those described in Robert Dahl (1977), p. 17.

page 37—"contain many relatively autonomous organizations": Robert Dahl (1983), p. 387.

page 38—"Pluralism I" and "Pluralism II": John F. Manley, p. 369.

Chapter 5: BUILD, MOP, and UNO

page 74—"enlightened understanding of [one's] best self-interest": Dahl (1977), pp. 11-12.

page 74—"It's the high you don't have to take drugs for": Chapter 2 of this book discussed Mancur Olson's theory of collective action, which proposes how unrealistic it is to expect people in most cases to contribute to the common good. He and others qualify that view in two principal ways. First, if the group is sufficiently small so that each member has some feeling of being necessary to the enterprise (it might not happen successfully without him or her), then it can be rationally, economically worth participating in the group if the results expected are clearly desirable. Second, there can be special incentives that have little or nothing to do with the more public question at hand. Olson calls these "selective incentives" because they have to work on the individual as an individual rather than as a member of the group.

   We have seen that the small scale and the purposes of community organizations are conducive to participation; they have Jefferson's prudent admixture of self-interest and public concern. In addition, they also have the advantage of many selective incentives, largely the kind Olson calls "social incentives." There are the joys of victory Ms. Montes is expressing here; the person-to-person relationships; the socializing, solidarity, and feeling of being an insider where the action is; the contacts with the outside world, and many other attractions that meet Olson's criteria. And he makes a special case for the federated type of structure that larger organizations such as BUILD, MOP, and UNO have, being made up of smaller autonomous units: "There is, however, one case in which social incentives may well be able to bring about group-oriented action in a latent group. This is the case   of a 'federal group'—a group divided into a number of small groups, each of which has a reason to join with the others" (Mancur Olson [1965], pp. 62-63).

It is more difficult to be optimistic about how community organizations overcome the limitations Arrow describes (chap. 2). A group of people at a community meeting often have as much trouble reaching a meaningful consensus as the picnickers do. But Arrow's application of the difficulty is electoral voting, and that does underscore a difference. Voting is an essential but very limited act; all you can do is mark your ballot in the space provided on the day specified and then live with your choice. It is indeed difficult to affect policy in any rational way with that vote. On the other hand, the community organization processes in this chapter are much more evolving, organic experiences in which, as noted, there is room for looking at the consequences of initial actions, modifying the strategies, moving ahead, and then learning again. The chance to have both individual and group interests articulated and applied over time is an advantage community organizations have in coping with the complications in group decision making that Arrow has identified.

Chapter 6: Roots of Our Habits

page 81—In Italy: The information on Italian philanthropy is from Richard C. Trexler, esp. pp. 64-75 and 100-103.

page 82—"If you want honor": Trexler, p. 101.

page 84—its cynicism about support from foundations and corporations: Since this was written, BUILD has asked for and received a $35,000 grant from the Morris Goldseker Foundation of Maryland for a new project organized around issues of public housing.

Two of the three community organizations described here have relied largely on sources of support other than foundations, corporations, and wealthy individuals. Church funds have been their main resource. As the church sources are the first to say, such funds are severely limited. For growth in the number of stable organizations and to ensure the improvements in compensation necessary to get and keep competent staff, participation from other sources of private philanthropy is essential.

page 84—the powerful livery companies: These organizations trace their histories back to the early Saxon guilds. They became the strongest expressions of private philanthropy in England, "giving financial help to liverymen and freemen experiencing hard times, or to the widows and children of deceased members." John Kennedy Melling, p. 10.

page 84—"The poorest class of society": A.R. Hands, pp. 89-91.

page 85—"Knowing the poor, the nonpoor extended charity": Alan B. Batchelder, p. 43.

page 85—as the poor became less frequently familiar neighbors. . ., they became instead "a social problem": David J. Rothman, p. 156. The emphasis on "neighbor" is significant. It seems clear that an important qualification about our early American good feelings was the distaste for "vagabonds" (Rothman, p. 5). As in England and elsewhere in our cultural history, charity was local assistance for those who belonged to the community. Strangers were distrusted and the poor among them sent on their way. Poor neighbors tended to be our genteel poor, while poor strangers were our "miserables," who perhaps had just as little charity available to turn to as did their fourteenth-century counterparts.

page 85—Here, as in Europe, hospitalization was originally only for the poor: In France, in the mid-seventeenth century, hôpitals meant workhouses for the poor rather than facilities dispensing medical services. Both Rothman and Paul Starr describe how America repeated the European experience of shifting medical services from home care to institutions, and doing it first for the poor, for whom such institutions were a form of incarceration. See Starr, pp. 148-151, 466n.; and Rothman, pp. 45, 190.

page 86—Although they have accepted some charity cases: Today, of course, third-party payments turn more people into revenue-producing patients, but insurance and public funds are the governing factor, not private philanthropy.

page 86—"the difference in economic level": William S. Vickrey, p. 44. It isn't as though there haven't always been impressive calls for attention to the poor from within philanthropy. This is from Richard T. Crane, founder of the Crane Manufacturing Co. in Chicago, in 1907:

"I have no quarrel with those who would make the city more beautiful than it is, but I would have all such schemes begin at the bottom. I would not put money into boulevards and statues, and fine bridges, and elaborate public buildings until the immediate surroundings of the poor are made better and decenter. . . .

"This is an age of great disparity between the rich and the poor. It is a time of much discontent among the latter, discontent that undoubtedly is justified, as they have not received their rightful share of the prosperity of the country. Consequently, when the time comes for dispersing large fortunes, the bulk of them should go to the poor. Instead of this we are hearing continually of large sums of money being given for purposes that can be of little interest to the poor, or of little benefit to them, and which mainly serve to gratify the vanity of the rich." Quoted in Wayne Andrews, pp. 162-163.

page 87—"One suspects that foundation grants": Kenneth Boulding and Martin Pfaff, p. 389. Private philanthropists should not be singled out for having the only giving habits that mostly support the nonpoor. As Gordon Tullock points out, we have our government make "massive redistributions" of resources in the United States, which "are not in the main transfers of funds from the wealthy to the poor, but transfers of funds among the middle class" (pp. 380-386).

Assistance to Families with Dependent Children is the major government cash assistance program for the poor. In 1984, after recent cuts, AFDC cost only 5 percent of the amount spent for Social Security. According to William O'Hare, "Most of the government outlays for social programs go to the elderly and middle class" (p. 25). There is even a "Director's Law" that says a disproportionate share of government expenditures primarily serve the more prosperous citizens. It is named for Aaron Director, who first made the observation when he noticed the expensive cars of people who were using our national parks.

page 87—A gift to a worthwhile organization "is no less generous": A point made by Morris Silver, p. 28.

page 87—Abraham Maslow: See esp. chap. 4.

page 88—their role can be recognized, appreciated, and encouraged: One needs to be sensitive, however, to the impact of organizing—and funding—on the decisions of families about whether to stay in a troubled neighborhood. In the worst scenario, those who profit from families staying are not the families themselves but the people who eventually come around and capitalize on what's left when the neighborhood's assets have become devalued. The families in such cases have been caretakers for the neighborhood, "neighborhood sitters," suffering its disadvantages while keeping some semblance of order intact until the area is turned into something else, which probably will displace the caretakers.

Again, community organizing is full of profound questions about human lives. It is great for organizing to help convince people to stay in a community and work right there for themselves and their neighbors. But in the actions and attitudes of leaders, organizers, and funders, as well as of the families themselves, that objective has to be balanced against a recognition of realistic opportunities that may more likely be available someplace else.

page 89—Harvard was not at all a private, independent institution: Data on Harvard and Yale support are from Peter Dobkin Hall, p. 108; see also pp. 194-195. For a description of how the private stewardship of social services worked out in a specific community, see Kathleen D. McCarthy.

page 90—"Even the charities of the nation": Letter to David Williams, 1803, in Padover, ed. (1939), p. 136.

page 90—There was a "vast surplus of wealth": Eduard C. Lindeman, pp. 4-5.

page 90—"If it is said that the nunnery": Trexler, p. 71.

page 91—a "mounting financial crisis": Martin Mayer, pp. v, 1, 98-99.

page 91—For-profit hospitals: A recent controversial analysis by Regina Hertzlinger and William Krasker lists the assumed virtues of not-for-profit hospitals and then claims that there are few such virtues, compared with for-profit institutions. Much the same type of analysis could be made in other traditional fields of not-for-profit activity currently being challenged by for-profit enterprise.

page 92—Figures on iatrogenic illnesses and injuries: According to an extensive government study of U.S. hospital records, 7.5 percent of all hospital patients suffer additional illnesses and injuries received while in the hospital. The report states that the data probably understate the true rate considerably. Leon Pocincki et al., pp. 73-89.

page 92—"to consolidate the nation's rich orchestra resources": Ford Foundation Annual Report (1966), p. 16. Also see the 1965 annual report, p. 32, and the foundation's separate report, 1974, pp. 48-49.

Barry D. Karl cited this experience in a talk before the Donors Forum of Chicago in about 1980.

page 93—"The Ford Foundation grants of a few years ago": Milton R. Bass quoted in Joan Simpson Burns, pp. 283-285.

page 94—"service delivery should not be based": Douglas Yates, p. 58.

page 94—what Barry Karl calls the popular "medical model" of philanthropy: The phenomenon is "deeply imbedded in the history of philanthropy in the form of the belief that all programs are inherently self-liquidating. Problems would be solved by sufficient money and brains, and the philanthropy would move on to other problems" (Karl, unnumbered).

page 95—grants for work against polio, typhoid: See, for instance, James A. Joseph (1983), p. 2.

page 95—The 1910 Flexner Report: Starr, pp. 118-121.

page 95—"hasten the abolition of international war": Carnegie Endowment for International Peace, p. 183.

page 95—"a pleasant philanthropic dew": Edwin Rogers Embree and Julia Waxman, p. 32.

page 96—"Foundations have a special opportunity": Embree and Waxman, p. 218.

page 96—a "problem statement or needs assessment" [and subsequent quotations]: Grantsmanship Center, pp. 1, 13, 20, 24.

Chapter 7: Politics and Altruism

page 100—limits that were clarified and liberalized by Congress in 1976: Lobbying by Public Charities, PL 94-455. In November 1986, the Internal Revenue Service released proposed regulations that would, it appeared, take a step in the other direction by introducing new ambiguities and limitations. Hearings, counterproposals, and discussions are continuing in late 1987. For up-to-date information, contact either the Council on Foundations or the Independent Sector (see app. II).

page 105—"democracy is based on the assumption": A.D. Lindsay, p. 33.

page 106—*prosocial* behavior is a relatively new and frequent term: See, for instance, Lauren Wispé, pp. 1, 11; and Paul Mussen and Nancy Eisenberg-Berg, p. 171.

page 106—"socially valuable but individually disadvantageous": David Layzer, P. 297, quoting the pioneer English geneticist J.B.S. Haldane.

page 107—good intentions are not enough: But they are essential. Without them, a giving program is shaky at best. As psychologist Ervin Staub says, "Someone who acted kindly for selfish reasons may act unkindly next time" (p. 138).

page 109—"It does not follow": Derek S. Wright, p. 127.

page 110—"recognize the other person's reality" [and] "It is a question not of compassion": Thomas Nagel, p. 83.

page 110—the "common public life" [and subsequent references]: Arendt, pp. 28, 30, 52, and passim, esp. in chap. 2.

page 110—"To help other men according to our ability is a duty": In Milo, p. 68.

page 111—"If a man practices it": Milo, p. 68.

page 112—Despite the presumptions: Evidence of contemporary development from these philanthropic roots is to be found in the results of a recent study by Teresa Odendahl of the creation and growth of foundations: "Of the twenty motivations for forming a foundation that were listed in the survey, the one that scored highest in intensity across all foundations was the donor's personal philosophy. It is one of a cluster of motivations. . .that seems to reflect altruistic sentiments. It includes a concern for the welfare of others, religious heritage, a belief in social responsibility, and a family tradition of charitable activity" (p. 78).

page 113—There are several possible points of entry: Altruism was once a major puzzlement in the study of evolution. Under the terms of survival of the fittest, why should a prairie dog sound a warning when it sees a coyote coming? The cry only calls attention to this heroic watchdog and tends to make it a victim. Survival would seem to call for a quiet personal retreat.

In 1964, English geneticist W.D. Hamilton led the way to a different understanding of what happens. Our focus should not be on whether the individual prairie dog survives but rather on what happens to the genetic pool of which his own genes are a part. If the prairie dog dies but in doing so at least temporarily assures the lives of several members of its family, its gene pool thrives. Families of prairie dogs that have the trait of sounding warnings will, over time, be the survivors.

Sociobiologists thereby find a friend in the nineteenth-century English author Samuel Butler, who decided that a hen is an egg's way of making more eggs. Thus also came the title of Richard Dawkin's book, *The Selfish Gene*, which has won a broader public for sociobiology. As the title implies, it is the gene's self-interest that is significant, not the person's.

Stimulating, understandable books in the field include those by Edward O. Wilson and David P. Barash, and two collections of articles: Michael S. Gregory et al., eds., and Elliott White, ed. Numerous controversies have arisen in response to sociobiology, particularly around Wilson's more dramatic conclusions. Some of the criticism is political, reacting to sociobiology's claims and inferences about genetic influences in our lives. Much of the scholarly criticism looks like social scientists, still smarting from the invasion from economics, now having to defend their turf against new inroads from a totally different direction. According to Garrett Hardin in Gregory et al., eds. (1978), "Their reaction to the appearance of sociobiology is a casebook study in territorial behavior" (p. 184).

In addition to its relevance to altruism, sociobiology also provides useful insights about the pluralist description of our society discussed here in chapter 2. It raises the question of whether we really can have the equilibrium that pluralism tries so desperately to achieve. As Kenneth Boulding points out in Gregory et al., eds. (1978), "the evolutionary approach to social systems...repudiates the concept of equilibrium and sees the world as a continuing ongoing flux that never repeats itself. ....*The world will change regardless of what we do about it. And we can put in our two bits' worth to divert the course of evolutionary change, as our understanding of it grows, toward the better rather than toward the worse*" (emphasis added) (p. 275-276). (That passage would look well on a philanthopist's letterhead.)

page 114—"Equality of condition": Alexis de Toqueville, vol. 2, p. 175.

page 115—"the welfare of individual members of the next generation is interdependent": Brian Barry (1978), p. 226.

page 116—"[A]ltruism survives because it enhances community cohesiveness": Shmuel Amir and David Bigman, pp. 56, 58.

page 116—"The presence and persistence of altruistic values": ronald Cohen, p. 52.

page 118—"In the language of game theory": Amir and Bigman, p. 64.

Chapter 8: How to Evaluate Proposals from Community Organizations

page 124—Are they able to raise some money in the community: Local church and business sources can yield considerable support. Expectations of funding from families and individuals, however, need to be modest.

One of the fund-raising limitations for many community organizations is that the individual churches, block clubs, school groups, and other neighborhood associations that make up the community organizations all have their own expenses to cover, through their own fund raising. There is also the competing need for money for political campaigns in the community. The relatively large community organization, which has more potential for getting new outside funds to help the community, may be justifiably reluctant to raise funds aggressively in the community because it would drain off modest resources available to member groups and to the campaigns of local candidates for elected office.

On the other hand, some activities, including "fund raisers" and benefits, are useful in getting people involved and in showing everybody—including outside funding sources—that the community supports its community organization. Money raised in the neighborhoods by members themselves—from among themselves directly and from those church, business, and agency funds that "belong" to the community—is the "freedom fund"; it is an effective working symbol of their independence and community control. The dream is always to create a for-profit venture that will support the organization. The record of realizing that dream in low-income communities is not good.

page 128—"the game *is* the candle": John G. Simon speaking specifically about foundation grants in the "public affairs" area, p. 99.

page 133—the foundation has to assume "expenditure responsibility": See Internal Revenue Code, Section 4945. See also David F. Freeman's valuable handbook, esp. pp. 35-40; and in Appendix 5, pp. 161-163, Freeman reprints a Council on Foundations memorandum on the subject and shows a sample letter to use in expenditure responsibility grant agreements.

page 135—so they will "behave well": M.J. Heale, P. 173. John W. Nason concludes his remarks to foundation trustees about "The Hard Choice Among Public Needs" by saying, "If too many people feel left out of the system, sooner or later they will seek to change the system. This is the stuff that revolutions are made of" (p. 28).

page 136—funding sources and other professional outsiders have long been guilty: Examples are familiar in the experiences of many community groups and funders. To quote Bob Nichol, former program officer of the Charles Stewart Mott Foundation: "The very availability of funds. . .has encouraged many community organizing efforts to get into the program operating and service delivery business. . . .This seductive pressure from funders, I believe, has diverted the energies of many community organizing efforts. . .from organizing to service delivery in order to hang on to foundation resources" (personal correspondence, 19 October 1983).

Occasionally the habit is reflected in print. Usually community organizing is given the role of being just the elementary first step toward something more attractive. Two examples, the first from Robert L. Woodson and the second from Philip Drotning:

> Research has shown that community groups pass through six distinct stages as they evolve. . .[from] The Ad Hoc Stage [where] concerned citizens come together to decide what needs to be done. . .and take action and disband when the problem has been resolved. . .[to] The Professional Stage [and] The Equity Stage [which is] the equivalent of institutional status. . . .These [final] enterprises often take the form of for-profit subsidiaries whose utility frequently outlives and overshadows the usefulness of the nonprofit parent organization in pure economic terms (pp. 146-147).

> Neighborhood organizations typically form around an issue, an issue so aggravating that people decide to join forces and try to do something about it. That is the activist period. . . .Eventually [the organization] will move to projects. . . .This is the point at which the organization maybe buys a building and tries to rehab it. . . .At the activist stage the organizations have very little outside financial support, nor do they need much. . . .When they get project-oriented they start needing professional staff. . . .Moreover, the more sophisticated they get about the projects the less attention they pay or need to pay to the activist aspect of their role (pp. 6-7).

The complaint of those of us who are dismayed by these attitudes is not that development work isn't important but rather that outsiders so often want to take community organizations, whose mission is participation, and say that if the organization is any good it will mature into some other sort of institution.

page 138—This was the theme of the 1986 Council on Foundations conference: See Joseph (1986), preface.

page 139—two strategies needed for generating stronger traits of altruism: Layzer, p. 303.

Chapter 9: Winning Effective Roles for Professionals in Communities

page 141—"Paradoxically. . .advocacy implies an essentially paternalistic attitude": Heinz Eulau, p. 187. For a provocative discussion of the problem, see also David G. Smith.

pages 141-142—a social worker. . .a lawyer. . .a planner. . .an architect: One other group deserves a note. Entrepreneurs who establish not-for-profit housing development corporations and, increasingly, not-for-profit economic development projects in poor communities have a difficult problem. They must either compete with for-profit companies, if there are any, or do work that for-profit firms think is infeasible. Yet in return for their "license" to operate as not-for-profit agencies and—among other things—be eligible for grants and contributions, they must listen to community interests and involve them and abide by them in ways that can become expensive. Otherwise, it is hard for the rest of us to consider them charitable organizations. Suggestions given in this chapter about advocacy activities, such as links between agency services and community organizations and the development of community leadership on agency boards, are especially relevant to housing and economic development initiatives.

page 145—The idea of increasing the community governance. . .can sound personally risky: Cf.: "The attempt to involve clients and the public in the decision-making activity of nonprofit organizations is not without considerable cost and risk. Many attempts probably will fail, many will lead only to frustration and decisional deadlock. But, given the right conditions, nonprofit organizations can provide highly effective arenas for public and client involvement; more so, perhaps, even than government and market sector organizations. Clients can participate effectively and productively in third sector activities; the gamble seems worth the risk." Richard L. Cole, p. iii.

page 146—"three legitimate concerns" of a professional: Smith, p. 226.

page 146—the usefulness of being "a consultant and an advisor": David Easton, p. 1060.

page 150—but it's organizing "from-the-top-down": From Michael Hayes in Cigler and Loomis, eds. (1983): "Most of these groups are staff organizations. . . . [quoting Jeffrey Berry] 'There are not even formal concessions to a democratic structure in a majority of [these] membership groups' " (pp. 113-118). The lack of structured accountability leaves public interest organizations open to challenge. One of the few times this vulnerability has been used against such organizations was when Judge John Sirica ruled that Ralph Nader could not give testimony in the public interest on behalf of his groups because there was no machinery by which Nader was elected and re-elected to leadership by a valid, voting membership. See Graham K. Wilson, p. 101.

page 152—working. . .to comply with the IRS stipulation: It should be noted that the IRS five-state rule applies only to private foundation grants being made to specific agency programs established to carry out voter registration activities. This does *not* prevent a community organization (which is not likely to be working in five states) from spending some of its time registering voters, nor does it keep a foundation from making a general support grant to such a community organization—or any grant other than one specifically earmarked for voter registration. For further information, see Thomas A. Troyer, and Ad Hoc Funders' Committee for Voter Registration and Education.

page 155—This is trickle-down philanthropy: Both types of agencies described here, "umbrellas" and support agencies, become what a new body of literature calls "mediating organizations" or "intermediary organizations." The following excerpts are from a good example of that literature, New World Foundation's *Initiatives for Community Self-Help*, which emphasizes the "extraordinary importance" of these agencies in helping community organizations:

> The visibility, sophistication and professionalism of intermediary organizations provide them with greater access to the foundation world than local groups. . . . As more funding sources assist the community self-help world, intermediary organizations should tend to benefit, through increased funding (p. 23).

> There is the need for active intervention by intermediate organizations as brokers and interpreters (p. 34).

> Funders who are reluctant to move directly into the support

of local groups could connect with any number of excellent intermediary organizations (p. 46).

Intermediaries should be available to serve as a funding buffer. . .accepting wholesale grants and retailing smaller grants to community groups (p. 67).

By their very nature, nearly all intermediary organizations, to a greater or lesser degree, play the role of broker between local self-help groups and outside officials, institutions, political leaders, etc. (p. 88).

It seems ironic that community organizations should be called "self-help groups" in remarks that, at the same time, say that such groups must rely on intermediaries for their effectiveness in both program activity and raising money. Eulau's remark about the patronizing role of advocates (p. 141 of this book) is clear in identifying how intermediaries position themselves to represent and legitimize organizations of community people. When there is an intermediary in funding, the livelihood of a community organization depends on the likes and dislikes of the intermediary. The funding source has abrogated its responsibility for selecting where its money goes. There is no learning experience for the funder or for the community organization, since they are separated by the "buffer" of an intermediary.

page 159—numerous researchers have created unreal distinctions between private and public interests: For instance, in the extensive research designs of Verba and Nie, people who contact government about practical problems and needs are assumed to do so individually only about "relatively narrow problems affecting their own lives. . .personal problems [rather] than. . .public ones." When people take initiatives together, on the other hand, they are assumed by Verba and Nie to be doing so for "general communal goals" about "social issues," acting out of a "sense of general contribution to the community." The authors note, "Problems are not so particular, . . . [and]they may indeed be general social problems of the community" (pp. 77, 86, 91n., 114, 281). There is a brief footnote recognizing part of the problem.

Furthermore, the list of types of organizations Verba and Nie used in the surveys, from which people were to choose the types of organizations they were involved in, seems heavily weighted toward those that are (1) not part of public life in poor communities, and (2) much more recreational, social, and cultural in their functions than concerned about basic needs of the members (table 2-2, p. 42).

page 159—so that unexamined premises won't "determine the selection of problems": Easton, p. 1058.

page 160—"I recognize": John L. McKnight, p. 15.

Chapter 10: Tracing the Initial Experience

page 165—A good book entitled *Doing Good*: Willard Gaylin et al., p. 95.

page 166—There were times in the 1960s and 1970s when students, members of the clergy, and other volunteers: VISTA volunteers, on the other hand, often were recruited from the community itself. The federal VISTA program was a valuable resource for those community organizations that used it; it was on-the-job training experience appropriate to community work.

Chapter 11: The Need To Trust the Public

page 178—*"Only when we start from a community as a fact"*: Dewey (1927), p. 149.

Paul N. Ylvisaker, once of the Ford Foundation and now a senior adviser to foundations for the Council on Foundations, gave his views on the present importance of local philanthropy in a talk to community foundation representatives: "This brings me to the easiest part of my talk: What's to do about it? Well, No. 1, take comfort in the increased recognition and saliency of your role. Much of the action is departing the national scene. It's no accident that Ford seems distant and drifting, that national foundations and their trumpets seem muted. Macro-solutions, whether in politics, economics, or philanthropy, have in their exhaustion given way to slogging it out problem-by-problem, community-by-community. Where it's at, is where you are" (p. 9).

pages 178-179—if we've learned anything about fixing our cities: Jane Jacobs.

page 179—*"intentional* altruism": Harvey Wheeler, p. 312.

pages 179-180—"mutually beneficial and mutually acceptable outcomes": Dahl (1978), pp. 201-203.

Index

ROBERT MATTHEWS JOHNSON is a staff consultant to the Chicago Community Trust and to the Gamaliel Foundation—a community organizing institute. For 15 years, he was the executive director of the Wiebolt Foundation where he established many of the principles associated with the funding of community organizations.